Heaven's Chancellery

Irina Zakirova

University Press of America,® Inc.
Lanham • Boulder • New York • Toronto • Plymouth, UK

4501 Forbes Boulevard, Suite 200, Lanham, Maryland 20706
UPA Aquisitions Department (301) 459-3366

10 Thornbury Road, Plymouth PL6 7PP, United Kingdom

Printed in the United States of America
British Library Cataloguing in Publication Information Available

Library of Congress Control Number: 2014945974
ISBN: 978-0-7618-6452-3 (cloth : alk. paper)—ISBN: 978-0-7618-6453-0 (electronic)

∞™ The paper used in this publication meets the minimum requirements of American National Standard for Information Sciences Permanence of Paper for Printed Library Materials, ANSI/NISO Z39.48-1992.

This book is dedicated to my dear parents Flora and Nicolay, who were brilliant teachers and will always be in my heart.

Contents

List of Characters

Adam – main character
Coeus – Adam's lawyer
Kumbi – the Judge
Vivimas – Siamese twin secretaries
Angela Phoros – the messenger from Heaven's Chancellery
Ipsos – the Prosecutor
Ptiscy – An angel who has trouble with flying
Themis – the goddess of justice
Arianna – the goddess of colors and emotions
Amaxas (Max) – the coachman
Granny-Boxes – the court audience
Cartoonist – the court cartoonist
Archio – Coeus' childhood friend; an archivist in Heaven's Chancellery
Komissa – Adam's adopted daughter; Countess

From the Author

When I began to write my doctorate dissertation regarding compensation for moral damage, some of my colleagues wouldn't agree with me that my idea would be significant. All of their skeptical remarks were mostly about: how is it possible to express ideas about non-material damage in a material form? However, to answer my dearest skeptics, after four years, my ideas about compensation for moral damage turned into physical forms: a thesis of my dissertation, 12 articles and a little brochure. Back then, I didn't even imagine that it would be my "cross" to carry for the rest of my life. Moral damage is affecting me even now; I became the bearer of moral damage. My colleagues who also wrote their dissertations with enthusiasm began to look like the bearers of their subject which they wrote about. One of them, who had done research about suicide, committed suicide. One candidate did research about vagrancy, and after he completed his dissertation, he felt such sympathy for vagrants that he became one of them and is currently nowhere to be found. That's the irony of researchers who have written their studies with great enthusiasm. My life has not been affected as dramatically as that of my colleagues. Having been affected by moral damage multiple times, I have never felt the satisfaction of having compensation for moral damage ordered by a court. But I have been multiple times compensated for this type of damage by various people, circumstantial events and maybe even mystical coincidences. I think that beneath all of this is a philosophical sense of the essence of moral damage which is impossible to completely compensate through the legal terms that have been used for centuries, which were created by people and are considered "from-this-world" civil laws. In this book, I present my own views of how moral damage can be compensated by having reality and mystery intervene in various life lessons.

Chapter One

Meeting an Angel on a Roof

The line to the small window was moving very slowly. Adam was moving his feet and throwing the pain in his legs from left to right. He still felt uneasy standing. The person who was standing in front of him was of a small height with a very smooth bald head. He saw how on the baldness sometimes appeared a few drops of perspiration because the air in the building was humid. Occasionally, the plump man would wipe off his sweat with a tissue and hesitate from tiredness and Adam would imagine that he was the one hesitating. The sweaty bald man was getting closer to the window and Adam was getting excited. Finally, the sweaty bald man disappeared and it meant that Adam could now hand in his petition. The woman accepted his petition, stamped his papers and after which he understood that he wanted to get out of this building as soon as possible. However, in front of the door saying EXIT, a yellow band of tape was hanging and because construction workers were walking there with dirty clothes that were filthy with dust, he understood that he had no chance of going out of that door. He had to look for another exit. One of the constructors showed him the stairs and Adam thought that he could only get to an Exit by going upstairs to the second floor and then going downstairs from another wing. He began walking up the empty stairs, but later he understood that there were no exits for the second, third or fourth floors. He only had to walk up and up and later he got curious about where the stairs might lead him.

"Maybe it takes me to the roof," thought Adam. "Well, I guess it's interesting to be on the roof of the Supreme Court building. Why not?" he asked himself.

Soon Adam reached the roof of the Supreme Court building. It was a smooth yard that had borders made out of bricks with sharp edges. He came up to one of the corners and with careful little steps and some curiosity, he looked down. People who were near the building were in a huge line, waiting to get inside the court building.

"Yep," laughed Adam. "All of these people are standing in line for justice, they probably chose the wrong door, just like me," he mused.

For some reason, he became very sad feeling, hopeless, he sat down on the corner of the roof. There was not even the slightest wind and the veins near his temples began pulsing again.

"My honor was defiled, my name was tarnished, my individuality was stepped on. Today it is almost three years since I walked in the building of the court and tried to get at least a cent for the moral damage that was imposed on me." He murmured skeptically, "Oh God, is it true there are no courts on earth which would at least listen to my story, to my case? Probably not. Maybe only heaven will able to compensate my moral damage."

Not a second passed before Adam heard a voice behind him. Adam turned around and saw a man in a weird angel costume. At first, he thought that he was hallucinating because he had been really sad and hadn't really been sleeping for a few nights and he supposed the angel would disappear in a few moments. He rubbed his eyes with his knuckles. However, when he opened his eyes, the angel was still there and was looking straight at Adam.

"Your statement was heard" the Angel said with a bored voice, "the members of heaven's chancellery are allowing you to submit a petition."

"To where?" Adam asked in bewilderment.

"To heaven's chancellery" the Angel repeated, "weren't you, a few seconds ago, complaining that no court that is standing on earth would hear your case? Now you have a chance for heaven's chancellery to hear all that you have to say."

Adam still couldn't believe what was happening. "You're saying that you are an Angel from heaven's chancellery?" Adam asked with a smirk.

"Yes, I am," said the Angel. "Sorry I didn't properly introduce myself when I just landed on this roof. My name is Ptiscy[1] And believe me, it is not that easy to land on such a small territory as the roof of the Supreme Court," he complained.

Adam studied the man who was wearing a cloak made out of white silky feathers.

"Oh, you must be an actor who dressed up as an angel and for some reason ended up on this roof, and you must have seen that I handed in my petition downstairs. Well, I'll tell you that it is not nice to make fun of me like that at all." Adam turned from Ptiscy.

But Ptiscy didn't get mad and said, "Well, ever since I started working as a messenger, for all the times I have come to people, I have heard many weird comparisons, but most often they say that I'm a hallucination, but I like your comparison of me being an actor as well," Ptiscy assured him.

Adam was chuckling and laughing with amusement. He turned to Ptiscy and decided to continue their conversation in the form of a play, so he asked,

"Well, tell me, Angel, how can I hand a petition to heaven's chancellery, if I don't even have a pen or a white sheet of paper, nor a computer to get the petition ready?"

To which the Angel calmly nodded his head and said, "Oh, this should not bother you at all."

He raised his hand and by pointing a finger, he began drawing a frame in the air the size of a sheet of paper, and the frame started glowing and looked like jelly that was hanging in the air.

"Here you go. You can write your petition here," Ptiscy said.

For the last three years, Adam had seen huge folders with thousands of paper petitions, but a petition on jelly paper overwhelmed him. Sweat started pouring down his body, even through his hair. He remembered the bald guy who had been standing in front of him in line. Adam gathered all of his bravery and touched the jelly-like paper with his finger. However, he didn't feel sensation on his skin.

Stuttering he asked, "Ho-w a—m I su—p-po-sed to w-ri-te on th—is?"

"We never take petitions in handwritten or typed forms, we believe that any petition should be written by the power of thought and soul," the Angel declared. "We don't review other petitions at our court. You should think of anything that you want to write in the petition and all of your thoughts will appear on this form."

The sweat on Adam's head evaporated and by taking slow steps he came closer to the hanging object in the air. He thought, "Petition from Adam," and actually a moving phrase began appearing on the form.

"So it is really real," Adam said in astonishment.

The Angel just shrugged his shoulders and looked at his watch.

"You should hurry," warned Ptiscy. "If you don't complete the petition, it will soon disappear, and I too have to go. The wind will be blowing soon and it's hard for me to fly during windy weather," said Ptiscy.

Adam quietly did what Ptiscy told him to do. Soon, the form, which was the size of a sheet of paper, was full and the petition was complete.

"How should I sign it?" Adam asked.

"As we usually do it in heaven, just touch it with your finger and it will mean that you are authorizing your petition," said Ptiscy.

Adam touched the form in the corner, and at that same moment the jelly form disappeared. Adam shivered and he again began to feel a shaky emotion from not understanding what was going on with him.

"Well, that was good," said Ptiscy. "And it's time for me to go now."

"W-e-ll, h-ow ab-o-ut m-e a-nd m-y p-eti-tio-n?" Adam asked.

"Oh, don't worry about your petition, our procedural terms are never violated, not like in the earthly courts," Ptiscy said superiorly. "Your case will be reviewed en banc court without any delays, there is no another way."

The Angel moved Adam to the corner of the roof and began to get his wings ready to fly.

"Don't worry too much," Ptiscy said in a friendly voice. "Millions of cases similar to yours were reviewed in our court and have had very successful endings."

"Whe…"Adam tried to ask.

"Ohh," answered Ptiscy, realizing what Adam was trying to ask, "you will receive the summons very soon."

Ptiscy got to the very corner of the roof's border with his bare feet and opened his wings to full length and Adam finally saw that it wasn't a cloak at all. Adam thought that Ptiscy's wings were so big and beautiful. He even felt how powerful they were when Ptiscy was trying them out for the flight. Adam with surprise was reviewing the bones and the way they were built on the Angel's spine. He saw that Ptiscy's shoulder blades were similar to a human's but yet had extra bones which were attached to the wings, and it seemed to him that on the wings there were veins and blood vessels like that of humans. Adam watched how Ptiscy tried to fly from the roof of the Supreme Court building. He saw how Ptiscy with a huge amount of power pushed himself from the edge of the roof, how energetically he extended the span of his wings in order to gain height. For a second, Adam thought that he saw that it was very hard for Ptiscy to start flying since all of his bones tightened up. Adam thought he saw that on Ptiscy's face sweat started coming out and he caught himself thinking that even for an angel it was hard to fly.

Finally, Ptiscy was able to raise himself in the air and Adam saw how energetically Ptiscy began to move his wings and how hard it was. Adam tried to calm himself down by going to that very corner and was even more astonished when he saw that where the Angel's feet were just standing a second ago, there were bricks that were partly broken and pieces of white feathers. He took the feathers in his hands, and rubbed them a couple of times in order to calm himself down by proving to himself that he was not going crazy. Then, when he looked in the sky, he saw not an Angel but a white bird getting smaller and smaller in the sky.

NOTE

1. PTISCY—derived from the Greek, means flight.

Chapter Two

Conflict with the Actor

Adam was still standing on the roof and looking at the white bird disappearing in thin air. Then he got his thoughts together and understood that he needed to get out of there. "Why did I go to the roof in the first place?" "What if then police saw me? I definitely don't need any problems with the law. But still, if I got up here, why did the actor get up here in an Angel costume…I have a brain, why did I let some actor laugh at my situation and send some fake petition to heaven's chancellery. Heaven's chancellery, ha, what a deceptive trick he made up… guess all artistic people are creative… but to have a soul and laugh at me like that…he is definitely not an angel but a joker, and a bad one. But even if he is an actor, how realistic his wings were, they had veins and blood vessels, I'm sure I saw them. And I saw, with my own eyes, how this angel flew away from the roof…oh, I get it," Adam continued as he was going down the stairs, "he is not just an actor but also a magician and a hypnotist…maybe he is unemployed, just like me…oh, maybe there must be a movie rolling somewhere near and the actor decided to get on the roof… No, this all sounds weird." Adam reached downstairs, went through the exit, got outside and started heading to the subway station.

"Oh, I was right." Adam saw near Collect Pond Park, there was a movie shooting. He saw movie cameras on wheels, a few actors, but it was hard for Adam to see what was really going on from afar. Adam came closer and saw that the set was surrounded by yellow tape and getting closer was impossible. He saw children who were standing next to the yellow tape who were waving and screaming something to the actors.

"What's the movie about?" Adam asked the children.

"About a tooth fairy," said one of the boys and pushed a toothless smile at Adam. "I saw a couple of tooth fairies already," he told Adam and pointed somewhere. "But they are not real," he told Adam with a serious face. "They are just actors who dressed up as tooth fairies. But at night, I had a real tooth fairy who came in my room, and put a dollar under my pillow."

Adam wasn't really listening to the boy because he saw that among the actors was a young man who looked just like the angel-actor he had seen on the roof. Adam waved at him, hoping that he would come up to him. Adam really wanted to talk to him again, to be sure that he was not going crazy and what he saw was just a case of hypnosis or something similar. However, the actor didn't really seem to notice Adam. Adam waved at him again—no reaction. "What's happening here?" he wondered and started to get angry. "Only a few minutes ago, this poor actor so kindly offered me his help, and played a scene in front of me, as if some heaven's chancellery can help, and he now acts as if he doesn't notice me." After a few minutes, Adam without thinking what he was doing, jumped over the yellow tape, ran to the actor and started ripping off his costume. All of this happened in a few moments. The astonished actor didn't know what to do. Security guards ran up to help the actor, a movie operator started calling 911, and they all screamed for Adam to stop.

"Take off your jacket," Adam screamed at the actor and started ripping his clothes. "Open up your arms," he continued. "I saw it, with my own eyes, your wings have veins like that of humans and they are attached to your bones."

The astonished actor just took off his clothes, spread out his arms, and it was obvious that Adam was not satisfied. Soon, the movie crew ran up to them and couldn't understand what Adam needed? The actor's clothes, or did he want him to take off his clothes and be embarrassed, or did he want to harass him? Soon enough, the police came and Adam was arrested for disorderly conduct.

Of course, in the police precinct no one believed his story about how he got to the roof of the Supreme Court building, met an actor there who was dressed up as an angel who had real wings; who took a petition from Adam on a jelly screen which was hanging in the air and which petition the angel promised to send to heaven's chancellery; then the Angel flew into the sky and disappeared in thin air. No one believed his story, and it even made everyone laugh, especially, the officers who were doing the booking. The officers only had one question for Adam, "why would you try to take off the actor's clothes. Did you want to sexually harass him?"

"No, of course not," Adam exclaimed and took his head in his hands.

"Then why would you try to pull off the actor's clothes?" the police officer asked.

"Because I wanted to see the formation of his shoulder blades," said Adam, "that's where the wings grow."

The police weren't surprised by Adam's answer and one asked if he was currently on any medication? Adam said he wasn't, but did confess that he hadn't slept for a few nights straight because he was worried about his petition in court. The police officer felt sorry for Adam and suggested he visit a psychologist.

By the evening Adam was released to go home. On his calendar was one more set date—to visit the criminal court for a hearing.

Chapter Three

The "Law-Abiding" Angel

"People say it right, trouble doesn't come singly," thought Adam. "After a series of civil cases, I am now involved in a criminal case…now I am a criminal and on the criminal path," Adam sadly continued thinking, "But I wasn't wishing anything bad for the actor…" Adam was lost in his train of thought and with eyes full of sadness and loneliness looked out the window. In the distance he saw white birds, flying carelessly in an endless sky, and Adam started arguing with himself again, "I really did see an angel flying from the roof. I am certainly not mistaken; as I see these birds right now…I did talk to him and heard his voice." Then Adam went and turned on the TV and watched NY1 where an announcer talked about the latest news of the day.

First she talked about the weather: "Today the northwest wind has suddenly increased and it is expected to continue till the end of the day…Now in tonight's news, in Central Park, a white male in his 30's was arrested. His height is 6'2" and he has light brown hair and blue eyes. The man was wearing an angel costume and was barefoot. His costume wings got stuck in the upper branches of a tree. People who were in Central Park heard someone moaning and went to get help. Soon on the scene, NYC firefighters, NYPD and paramedics rushed to help the man to get down from the tree. Fortunately, the man was not injured; however, after he was brought down, he tried to flee the scene and knocked down a few people in the crowd that had gathered. The police asked him to halt, but he still tried to run off. Then the police used the TASER as the man appeared violent. Then the police took the man to the precinct, where he is currently located. After the interrogation and booking which the police conducted, two interesting things came out. He says his first name is Ptiscy, but he doesn't remember his last name. The man's name was not found in the U.S. search database nor were his fingerprints."

Adam watched with astonishment the scenes on TV and guessed he was the only one in the city to understand what had really happened down there. Adam sat on the couch and said only one thing, "Poor Ptiscy didn't have time to fly away…because the winds changed…" Adam's face changed, his eyes narrowing as they usually did when he was upset about something and he thought, "Because of me there is now another criminal case."

Adam turned up the volume and listened to the news woman more attentively. She was saying, "We have asked the commander of the central park police precinct to comment." The police commander was standing there and in the background were firefighters running back and forth with not just ladders but also with hoses, though there was no fire. There were police officers who were putting up yellow tape and were asking people to not crowd the incident scene. The commissioner said that the police officers of their precinct were doing everything possible to identify the man that they were able to save. The photos of this man would be sent to other precincts so that someone could identify him, because the man didn't remember his name, how old he was, and couldn't name anybody who knew him. The commander laughed and added, "The only thing the man said he knew was that he is a messenger from heaven's chancellery and that he came on earth with a special mission, to take a petition from a plaintiff for his case to be reviewed in the seventh level of heaven's chancellery. We don't know how this will help the investigation, but the man complained that the roof of the Supreme Court building is very uncomfortable and small, and it's hard to land on it or to have any justice. The man refused to explain how he got so high on the tree. He said the winds changed, and he took the wrong course and got stuck in the tree while trying to fly past it. I would also like to note that unfortunately, for the last 24 hours, this is the second time there a man arrested wearing the costume of an angel. In the morning, near the Supreme Court, a man tried to publicly undress an actor who was dressed as an angel while he was on a movie set. The man tried to take off his clothes and looked for wings on his shoulder blades. After which he was arrested. He too was saying something about angels and heaven's chancellery." Then the commander asked anybody who was able to identify this man to call the number on the screen. When Ptiscy's photo appeared on the screen, Adam was already putting his jacket on and, without turning off the TV, rushed outside.

When Adam was on his way to the precinct to help out Ptiscy, he felt very sorry for not having wings and not knowing how to fly. Not remembering how, he reached the precinct and after a few hours he was standing in front of the officers and tried to tell them that he personally knew Ptiscy, and could pay the bail for him. Ptiscy, who was then taken out from the cell, looked very pale, lost and sorry for what happened. His shoulders, which were bearing the wings, were hanging down like two broken hangers. Adam noticed that when he saw Ptiscy the first time he was holding his wings with pride, but now they were just hanging down and seemed heavy. But to be polite, he smiled at Adam as if they had known each other their whole lives and he tried to find understanding in Adam's eyes. For some time, Ptiscy and Adam were silently just staring at each other, as if they were mind-reading. They both understood that if they told the truth, they would be spending more time in the police precinct. Plus, Adam for some reason really wanted to have proof that Ptiscy was the unemployed actor, so that he wouldn't feel that he was getting crazy. That's why when Ptiscy was offered a plea bargain, Adam was for it. He started telling Ptiscy what he had to say.

As a result, after a few hours, the judge was listening to the following explanation from Ptiscy: "I am Ptiscy, an unemployed actor. I don't have a prior criminal record. I was very upset that I didn't have a job and that's why in Central Park, I myself climbed up the highest tree to cope with my stress and in this way I scared people in the park. When the firefighters took me down from the tree, I was very embarrassed that I did such a dumb thing and that's why I wanted to run away, so that people wouldn't laugh at me. I accidentally hit a few people in the crowd, but I didn't mean any harm. That's why I wanted to run away as far as I could from my embarrassment and didn't hear when the police asked me to stop. I ask for forgiveness from everybody whom I caused harm. I am guilty." After some time, a police officer came in and started mumbling something to the counsel who was representing Ptiscy. The police officer came out and the counsel murmured very quietly to Ptiscy, "Two weeks ago there was a robbery of a Party City store, $535 was stolen, a helium machine for blowing balloons, and four costumes, two of them of pigs, one of Barney and one of a Minnie Mouse. Say that you stole them." Astonished, Ptiscy looked at his court-appointed lawyer and said that he of course didn't do that, because he didn't wear costumes. He never wore costumes and didn't plan on wearing any costumes in his life. To which the lawyer said, "You don't have to wear the costumes, but it's better to say that you did it."

"Why?" Ptiscy asked quietly; to which the lawyer answered, "Because after half an hour you will be free, you silly, and I have lunch very soon and then I gotta go to other four precincts later in the day." It seemed that Ptiscy couldn't understand what his lawyer was talking about, though he very enthusiastically continued, "Yesterday, I bought new shoes, and I'm wearing them for half a day. My feet are killing me, I have bloody blisters." For Ptiscy to believe him, the lawyer put his foot up on the table and pulled down his socks. Ptiscy did see blood on his lawyer's feet. Ptiscy pitifully looked at the blisters and shyly looked at his barefeet and for some reason, in agreement, nodded his head and said, "Yes, I am guilty of that too." "Good," said the lawyer. "I think the judge will able to make a just decision." When the decision of Ptiscy's freedom was ready and signed by all sides, Ptiscy even refused to take the copy of the paperwork. He hurried outside with Adam and said only one thing, which only Adam was able to understand, "The wind has begun to change. I have to go."

Near the precinct doors, Adam and Ptiscy weren't standing for long. It was obvious that Ptiscy was rushing and every second was gold for him. Meanwhile, Adam was again in confusion. On the one hand, he wanted to prove to himself that Ptiscy was an actor, but on the other hand, he again saw that the structure of Ptiscy's shoulder blades was different from that of humans. Then, Ptiscy headed forward to the bus stop because it was the only way to get away from this place. However, Adam noticed that no bus or cars were moving, the streets were empty, and Ptiscy was already gone in an instant.

Full of doubt, Adam returned home and saw that the TV was still on. The same channel was talking about the news for the night. This time, in the studio, there was the governor who was giving an interview regarding the latest series of arrests involving people dressed up as angels. The governor was saying something for a long time about the upcoming election and about a new program of the candidates for a new governor. He stated that it all was a trick by one of the election campaigns, specifically, that of his opponent. He added that most likely that new candidate, among other promises in his program, had mentioned one of the major goals, one of which was to reform the judicial system. He even brought flyers of his opponents where it was written, "Today's judicial system is rotten, today the courts are crowded. They are filled with technical mistakes and unjustified solutions. Hundreds of innocents who are incarcerated and their families and friends are suffering because of this. Sometimes, the current judicial system due to its mistakes creates new criminals. Today, the time has come to end this! Join us and you'll save thousands of innocent lives!"

The governor assumed that this candidate hired actors in angel costumes to protest against the judicial system. The angel costumes, in his opinion, symbolized heaven's chancellery, which was pure and just, and if people followed the new candidate, then they would be able to reform the current judicial system.

Adam was quietly listening to the whole interview, and was surprised how the media twisted the information and was even trying to make money and publicity. In a few minutes, breaking news came up, and as affirmation to the governor's interview, one of the reporters commented from the scene. He stated that a few hours ago, in the Bronx, a group of young people were stopped who were all dressed up in angel costumes. They were walking around the streets and were loudly screaming and singing. When the journalist tried to interview them and asked, "You came out to protest against the rotten judicial system..." one of the young people took away the microphone from the reporter, made crazy faces at the camera, gave it the finger and said, "The f*** with your judicial system. No one f***ing cares about it."

The reporter wanted to redirect the interview and said, "You are probably supporting the new program of the candidate who's running for governor. You support the movement to have the courts be more just to the people."

One of the protestors burped in the reporter's face and said, "Everything's cool. We're just having some fun. What court are you talking about? We're coming from a bar, and you're talking some crazy sh** about some court"

Then he tried to take away the reporter's microphone and sing a song. Then the camera fell to the ground, it seemed that they started fighting, and then the breaking news ended.

"What did I get myself into?" thought Adam. "I would give everything I have to know what will happen next..."

Chapter Four

Angela Phoros Brings the Summons

Over the next few days, Adam was constantly arguing with himself, and finally concluded that his meeting with Ptiscy on the roof was just a dream. He even went up to his attic and found one of his grandfather's old books about psychology. He sat down on the floor and he didn't even mind that everything was dirty and covered with dust. He started skimming through the book and trying to find something relevant for him. Finally, he found a paragraph in which it said that after a severe nervous shock, a person may expect hallucinations which will seem very real to him. Reading this paragraph, Adam felt a certain relief and even happiness that there was a reasonable explanation as to what had happened to him a few days ago on the Supreme Court roof. At this point he realized that the feathers which he picked up on the roof of the Supreme Court building must have been the feathers of a white bird. Happily he came down stairs and decided to take a shower. When he felt the fresh water on his skin, it finally relieved him. And then when he was shaving, he realized that he had a look of relief in his eyes. He even started smiling, but after a few moments he saw a reflection of a silhouette. He heard a voice behind him: "Adam, here is your summons to heaven's chancellery."

He turned around with astonishment and saw a woman in her mid-50's who was dressed up just like the actor on the roof. She too had a cloak made out of silky feathers. The only difference is that her costume was of a light blue color and on her neck was a necklace which had a huge letter "M." He covered his eyes with his hands, and then he looked at his hands and one of them had a white cream on it. He again got scared as to why his hand had cream on it; it took him a second to realize that it was shaving cream. As he was looking at his hand with the cream, he asked, "How did you get here? I remember I closed the door."

The woman who seemed to be an actor wasn't surprised and said, "As usual, I flew in from the window."

"Flew in?" asked Adam as he was washing the cream from his hand.

"Well, yes. My flight here was very easy because of the tailwind."

"You actors have annoyed me to death for the last several days. Why are you after me? How did you get into my house? This is my house. Get out!" Adam screamed.

He kept yelling at the woman to get out and went to open the door. "If you won't leave, I'll call the police."

He picked up the phone and the woman began repeating his phrase, "My honor was defiled, my name was tarnished, my individuality was stepped on…"

Adam put down the phone and with astonishment started nodding his head, "Oh, that actor on the roof and you must be swindlers. You guys work together. Who are you? What's your name? But what do you want from me? You've got the wrong person, I don't have a lot of money."

"Well, my name is Angela Phoros[1] and I am the messenger from heaven's chancellery. Look, I even have this very special medallion which I received many centuries ago from the head of chancellery himself. To prove that I am not a swindler I absolutely know that when I fly away, you'll go back to the attic and look for that same paragraph in your grandfather's book which is on page 17, third paragraph from the top, in order to calm yourself down and conclude that I was just a hallucination."

Adam moved closer to the wall and sat down on the floor, not feeling his feet. He felt as if he was turning white. So many thoughts went through his mind that he couldn't analyze even one of them. He couldn't understand where the floor and the ceiling were.

The woman was satisfied with the fact that at least she was able to shut him up and finally give him his summons.

"Alright then, here is your summons, and considering your state right now, someone will be here to pick you up at the day of the hearing."

Once again, a jelly screen was hanging in the air in front of her. She said, "You have to sign here, dear. You already know how, don't you?"

Adam slowly touched the screen with his index finger and as before, at the same moment, the screen disappeared. He saw that on the summons, on the petitioner space, his name was written with beautiful script. On the very top where the name of the court usually went it was written "Seventh Level of Heaven's Chancellery." However, when Adam looked for the date and time of the hearing, there was a strange phrase, "When the winds will change." He blankly looked at Angela Phoros as she told him, "Well, I have to fly now, while there is still a tailwind. Once when I lingered with one of my very stubborn clients, I couldn't go back up. I had to wait out the night with a group of saints who were very welcoming and offered me one of their mattresses and a corner on 50th Street just behind the Saks 5th Avenue store. You must know where that is. Well, if you happen to be around that corner, would you mind saying hi from me to them?"

Adam looked at her and scoffed, "Do you know how expensive Saks 5th Avenue is? I wouldn't even able to afford their toothpicks. I bet those saints of yours have more money than I do, since they live next to it."

At this point Adam caught himself thinking that he didn't want her to leave. He wanted to talk to her even more. But as he looked up at her, he saw that she was standing barefoot on the windowsill. He then started remembering that the angel from the roof, Ptiscy, had also been barefoot. With astonishment he was watching how Angela Phoros spread her wings and how even the room started gleaming with a light blue color; he finally saw how beautiful his room was. Adam returned to his normal self and rushed towards the woman. Not wanting her to leave, he asked, "How am I supposed to get up there to heaven's chancellery?"

To which Angela Phoros gave a little smile and said, "Well, I hope you are not sensitive to flying on a coach convertible?"

She pushed herself from the window and was lightly moving her wings. Adam ran up to the window and saw that his new accomplice was looking like a huge blue bird flying further away. He saw a couple of blue feathers lying on the windowsill, but he did not pick them up. He absolutely knew that he was ready for his amazing journey yet to come…

NOTE

1. ANGELIAFOROS—derived from the Greek, means messenger.

Chapter Five

Ride on a Phaeton

Adam wondered what the next representative from heaven's chancellery would look like and where he would come in from. He looked out the window for the next few days but he didn't see anybody out there. Every time when he shaved, he would turn around to look if there was a messenger standing behind him, but no one was there. One day he even shaved only one cheek and purposely didn't shave the other in the hope that the messenger would come up from behind him, but still he was alone. On the seventh day when Adam stopped hoping and wasn't very nervous, he heard a voice from the window. It was coming from the kitchen.

"Mr. Adam, the coach is ready."

Adam went to the kitchen and saw how in his backyard a coach was hanging in the air with three giant white horses and an elderly man who was reining in the horses. As he was seeing this moment, he remembered that when he was buying this house, the real estate agent joked and said that even if it was a beautiful house, it had such a small backyard that even a horse wouldn't fit there. Adam laughed to himself and thought, "Ha, I wonder what face the real estate agent would make if he saw that in my backyard I don't just have a horse, I have three horses and a chariot with the coachman."

As Adam was laughing at his silent joke, the elderly coachman kindly said, "You should hurry up. I cannot hold onto an expansion of a narrow space for long. It takes away my energy."

"I will be ready in a couple of minutes," said Adam. "By the way, what a beautiful coach. I once saw a similar one in an old picture."

"This is not a coach," the coachman exclaimed. "This is a Phaeton, heaven's chariot. The most prestigious transportation between heaven and earth," the coachman proudly pointed out.

Adam was dressing in a hurry, without really noticing that he had his tie wrongside out.

"You said this is the most prestigious transportation. Which ones are less prestigious?" Adam was curious.

"Well, there is also Pegasus, which can transport you from earth to heaven and vice versa. But he is not as comfortable as a Phaeton, since it is known for making risky turns which makes people nauseated and they would even throw up right before their hearing," said the coachman.

Adam was standing in front of the window and was ready to climb on the Phaeton just like for a court hearing. He wore a white shirt and black pants and a tie which he still didn't fix. He climbed on the windowsill and continued talking to the coachman.

"Why was I given the honor to ride in the Phaeton?" asked Adam.

"Well, it's because you are going to seventh heaven, and the Phaeton always goes there. Am I missing something? Let me check," said the coachman. He took out his jelly pad, which didn't surprise Adam anymore. He started turning very thin pages and said, "No, I am right. Adam is to be delivered to seventh heaven for a case regarding the compensation for moral damage," the coachman assured him.

Adam took only one step and was instantly inside the Phaeton. The coachman kindly smiled, offered his hand and said, "By the way, my name is Amaxas[1] , but you can call me Max." Then he raised his jelly pad and said, "Sign here, please. I need you to authorize that I picked you up on time."

After that, what happened to Adam was in no way to be explained logically. The Phaeton rose smoothly over his house, circled around it and the street, then over the city, and was going higher and higher. Later, Adam saw roofs of the houses, green stains of parks and small rivers which looked like blue belts. Adam really wanted to memorize the road to heaven, so he would try to capture little images in order to remember where he was going. That's why he asked the coachman to drive a little slower, to which the coachman laughed and said, "Oh, my friend. Don't even try to memorize the road to seventh heaven. When you are going back home, you will be taken by a different route."

"How am I going to get back?" Adam asked with a little fear.

"Oh, don't worry about that," said the coachman swinging his hand. "There are many ways of coming back and the court will decide on that. Just enjoy the ride for now."

Adam leaned back, closed his eyes and fell asleep…

NOTE

1. AMAXAS—from the Greek, meaning coachman.

Chapter Six

Meeting Themis

Adam opened his eyes, and stepped out of the Phaeton. The first thing that he saw was a huge, gorgeous building with dazzling white purity. Standing on the sides of the building were two white columns. There was a beautiful long trail of stairs leading to a huge door. It was surprisingly quiet and when he was climbing the stairs, he could only hear his steps. He turned back to see if Max was still there, but he and the Phaeton were already gone. There was no one around. As he was climbing the stairs, it seemed endless, as if he was walking into the sky. He finally reached the door, and as he looked up, he saw a sign just above the door, "Temple of Justice."

As he was admiring the structure of the building, he realized that there was no door knob. He wondered how he would enter the building. He got closer to the door, and in a moment it opened itself. He made a step inside and saw a huge hall; it was pure white and Adam thought that he even saw sparkles of cleanliness. In the middle of the hall there was a huge glassy cylinder that Adam concluded was an elevator.

As he was planning to go towards it he heard steps from the other end of the hallway; he turned and saw a beautiful woman coming towards him. He got a little bit calmer since now he wasn't alone. The woman seemed to be in her 40's. Her dress was a simple white and loose-fitting. The fabric was draped in such a way that it emphasized her beautifully formed breasts. She had huge green eyes, brown curly long hair and as she was coming closer she was smiling. As the woman came up to Adam, he noticed the scent of an ocean breeze which was coming from her and she said, "I am Themis,[1] I have been waiting for you."

"I a-m Ada-m," he tried to say. At this moment he heard how his heart-beat was getting louder. He even thought that as if the whole building heard it and was beating just like his heart. He even felt embarrassed. He saw how this woman was very naturally sexy and gorgeous.

"I know," shortly answered Themis as if she heard what he was thinking.

To which Adam blushed and looked away and then said, "Themis…Themis, oh, you are the goddess of justice. I pictured you quite differently."

"Oh, yes," Themis laughed and the sound of her laughter seemed to echo across the whole building. "For all of these centuries, I have seen so many absurd images of myself created by you people."

Adam wanted to add something relevant and said, "Yes, usually near the front door of the court, I see a statue of you and here there are no statues at all."

Themis started laughing even more and exclaimed, "You people are so funny. Why do you think that putting a statue of me near the entrance of the court will make the trial absolutely fair? Believe me, for the trial to be fair, no statues are needed," she said as she shook her curls. And why would I put a statue of myself in my own house, since I am present myself and can change the course of justice as opposed to standing like a rock. Though most leaders do like to have statues of themselves, that's because they want their true selves and intentions to be hidden in a piece of rock," she finally said.

"Oh, well then, I can't really argue with that. But you know no one can really stop them doing all those sorts of things," Adam said

Themis looked at Adam and said, "We don't usually deal these sorts of cases here. There is a totally different place for people like that and a different elevator that goes downward. Though their cases are resolved much quicker than here, I usually don't like to go down there, because the justice that is being served can be disturbing. However, sometimes I do not have any other choice but to be present there."

"But where are your attributes? Your sword and shield, scales and a blindfold?" Adam asked, wanting to impress her with his knowledge of her.

But Themis was not impressed and on the contrary said in a serious voice, "Well, the sword and the shield, I have never carried. When my image was getting created and a photo session was done, the image maker took a sword and a shield from some warrior and took a photo of me with them, but then the Creator didn't like the image and he said that justice should not look like a soldier fighting a war, because justice has different tools for getting justice, so I have never held a sword and a shield since then."

"But you do have the scales and the blindfold? Right?"

"No, I don't," Themis said as she was playing with her dress. "I used to like to play with scales when I was a child, on the beach, placing sand in cups. By the way, my childhood friend Luitprand,[2] when he grew up, created an hour glass. He once told me that I inspired him to create them. At first it was my idea of measuring time by the flow of sand. In regards to the blindfold, when I was young, my curls were growing so fast that they were always in my eyes, so I thought of having my scarf around my hair, and sometimes it used to fall on my eyes. I remember how paparazzi, whom I think are as old as the creation of the world, took a picture of me with my scarf on my eyes and then the photo was spread around the world. As you see, I am not blind, not at all."

"So I guess you never judged with closed eyes, having scales to measure where truth and lies are."

"Of course not, there are no scales in the universe that would measure where is truth and lies with absolute exactness. And at any trial, the case should be judged with wide open eyes. A blind judgment is very dangerous."

Adam saw how Themis went towards the elevator and started pressing buttons. He looked at her beautiful silhouette and followed her.

"I don't like such symbols," Themis continued. "You people view symbols and attributes differently. That's why I rarely go down to earth's trials."

Adam wanted to ask more questions but Themis turned her head and said,

"It's time for you to go to your level of heaven's chancellery." She encouraged him to enter the elevator. "Press number seven and I'll see you there very soon"

For some reason, Adam didn't want to leave, he wanted to stay and talk to Themis about any subject that might pop up. He realized that she was quite appealing to him and he thought that once this was over, he would definitely find her again.

NOTES

1. THEMIS—the Greek Goddess of Justice.
2. LUITPRAND—the English scientist who invented the sand clock.

Chapter Seven

Strolling around Heaven's Chancellery

However, before Adam could press the button to reach the seventh floor, the elevator started moving by itself and by the beaming buttons he saw that he was moving lower and lower and finally reached level 1. The doors opened and two young men wearing boy-scout uniforms flew into the elevator and said, "Welcome to the distribution section!"

Adam tried to say that he wasn't going to the first level, but before he could say that, they took him by the arms and pushed him out of the elevator. Adam was able to just see that the elevator was already going up, and he wondered how would he able to go to the seventh level as Themis told him.

However, the two guys didn't leave Adam alone and even when he tried to tell them that he wasn't supposed to be there, they still stuck to their own thing and kept saying that any person, who reached heaven's chancellery, would always start their journey from this level. Later, Adam saw a long hallway and both walls were lined with chairs. People of various ages, genders, cultures, nationalities were sitting on them. Adam was also asked to take a seat and patiently wait to get called. Adam didn't like this whole procedure to just wait, because he hoped that once he'd get called to enter the white doors at the end of the hallway, then he would be able to explain that he was on the wrong level. He took a seat next to a man in his 50's, bald, and looked very much like that bald man who he stood behind in the line at the Supreme Court. It was obvious that the man was upset as he turned to Adam and said, "Can you believe it, the cases of my category have to be reviewed immediately. I cannot be waiting in a line." He was holding a big folder in his hands.

"What category is your case?" asked Adam, to seem polite.

"I am wrongfully convicted. I was locked in prison for 18 years and my case goes to level 3 miscarriages of justice court."

Adam couldn't understand what his neighbor in line was talking about, but he guessed that there was nothing to be done, but just to wait in line.

"But can you believe it. I have spent a handful of time in prison already, I cherish every minute of life that I still have. No one will able to return to me the years that I lost. Why do I have to waste my time here in the distribution level? They are all just dumb here. By the way, I'm Peter."

Oh, I agree with you, Pete," said a woman who was sitting on the other side from Adam. She was very plump, and didn't have a waist. "I also heard that angels who work here are the ones who are not highly qualified. They either are just starting their careers on this level, or they are brought here from upper levels as punishment."

"Why do you think so?" asked Adam.

"Because with my case, everything is also mixed-up," she said. "I was a victim of domestic violence a couple of times. My case had to be reviewed on the 5th level, the family court. But some dumb angel who I met in the elevator said that my case would be reviewed on the 6thlevel, the criminal court."

Then the woman who was sitting on the opposite end and had a cast on her arm said, "I have a similar case, I also thought that I'd be on the 5th level. But I heard that a new policy came out and no matter how much I love my husband and have asked the angels; because I faced a felonious assault, the case will be reviewed on the 6th level."

"This is absurd," said the plump woman. "This is my husband's and my business. In any case, I think it's better to review such cases in the family court. Why do they have to involve the criminal court?"

"What level do you have to get to?" asked the bald man from Adam

"Themis said I have to get to the seventh level" said Adam.

"Oh, wow," Adam's new acquaintances started saying and were looking at Adam differently. "Oh, my friend, you reached the top," they excitedly said. "It's rare for anyone to get to that level."

"I even heard that if you get the chance to win the case, you'll get an amazing compensation. But I petitioned for them to review my case, but they rejected it," said the plump woman

"They rejected me too," said the one with the cast.

"My question about the compensation was already approved in the earthly courts," said the bald man who was wrongfully convicted. "I already received my $1.5 million."

"So, now you don't have a chance to go to the seventh level? But you were wrongfully convicted?" argued both women.

"Unfortunately, not. I didn't know anything about the seventh level of heaven's chancellery when I gave in my petition on earth. I already received my monetary compensation, that's why heaven's chancellery will never take my petition." "So this is what it is, my brother," said the bald man and turned to Adam. "You gotta choose, it's either money from earth, or gifts from heaven."

At this moment, there was some kind of noise and a man was walking down the hallway and had a little monkey on his shoulder which was laughing and showing its pink butt to everybody. He was carrying a pot with a plant in his hands, he looked very tired. He had hair to his shoulders which were not washed and he wasn't shaved. The monkey was making loud noises, but the man for some reason was not bothered by it at all.

"Who is that?" Adam quietly asked his acquaintances

"Guess one of the representatives who's trying to get to the 2nd level, the environmental court. There are many of people like him here." said the plump woman.

They all got quiet because the man with the monkey sat next to them and patiently waited to get called. He looked very calm and wasn't worried that he got to the 1st level as opposed to everybody else.

"I warned people many times so that they wouldn't move the city close to the ocean," said the man with the monkey with a sad voice.

Adam and his acquaintances only quietly listened to the man and were watching how the monkey was sitting on his shoulder and twisted her tail around his neck.

"People don't understand. The wave needs a distance to come out from the ocean from time to time. No one listened to me, and now see what happened."

"You mean Hurricane Sandy?" asked Adam

"Yes, so many lives were lost, just because of human narrow-mindedness," he sadly concluded.

"What are you waiting from coming here?" the plump woman asked him.

"Honestly, I don't know what to wait for. Guess I'll be continuing to fight for the ocean shore to be farther from the city where people live. Nature has other laws, the ocean will be fighting for its territory and breaking everything in its way. It doesn't care how expensive the properties are. Fortunately, nature is not under the power of money."

"Oh you mean raising the tax for flooding?" curiously asked the woman with a cast.

"Not just that. Also that the flooding zone will be expanded further into the city," said the man with a monkey. "Believe me, nature's policies are stronger than any other policies."

As the time passed by, all of Adam's acquaintances as well as the others in line were getting to the white doors one after the other. Soon Adam was the only one sitting in the hallway. A worker from the 1st level came out from the white doors and carried folders. Adam thought, "How weird, an angel but without wings."

"Oh, I'm working on that for a second year now. It's no time for me to get the wings yet" said angel to Adam "But what are you still doing here," he asked Adam worried. "All distributions are finished for today."

"I told to your co-workers that as well, I don't have to be here" said Adam.

"Let me check all the folders before I take them to the archive," said the angel. After a few minutes he said, "Yes, you shouldn't have come here because I don't see your folder here. Oh, I think I know what happened. We recently hired new angels on internships and they all have to show a record of bringing people to our level. I apologize for the inconvenience; they shouldn't have brought you here. Come, let me walk you to the elevator"

After a few minutes Adam got in the elevator, pressed 7th button and slowly was going up.

However, Adam was soon stopped on 4th floor. He waited for a few minutes and then noticed that in the elevator was a phone. He picked up the phone and thought that maybe he'd reach an operator. A raspy voice was on the other end, and the operator said that the elevator was broken and that Adam should come out from the emergency exit door in the elevator. Adam came out and understood that for some time he will have to spend time on this floor, before the elevator would be fixed. As he came out he saw the same hallway as on the 1st level, with the exception of chairs. The hallway had a long carpet which led to a huge white door. Adam had nothing to do but to follow the carpet. It seemed to him as if he was walking in an official organization. Truly, when he came closer, he saw that above the door was a sign, "Cost-Analysis Court." "Interesting, I have never thought for such court to exist," thought Adam. "Well, you could only expect that from heaven's chancellery," he concluded.

However, when he came in through the doors, he didn't see an ordinary space as is usual in courts. There were no special desks for the judges, the counsel and the prosecutor. The space mostly looked like a conference room, similar to the one in his university. The room had a lot of chairs, probably placed for a big audience. What surprised Adam the most was that the place where usually a presentation board was placed was a big jelly screen. Almost the same structure as Ptiscy had it but much bigger and thinner. Adam thought that movies were probably shown on this screen.

"Yes," he heard a voice saying behind him. "Only not just plain movies, but movies of life."

Adam turned around and saw a woman in her 60's with white, snowy hair and maybe because she was wearing glasses her expression looked especially wise.

"Let me introduce myself," she said and offered her hand at Adam, "My name is Oscar. For many centuries I am the head of this court level."

Of course Oscar wasn't the head of the court level from birth. When she lived on earth, she used to be one of the famous movie producers. People say she made great movies; however, no matter how many times the movie got nominated, she never won the longed for statue. She was very worried about it and started drinking alcohol. Once after a long depression and long drinking of alcohol, she died. When she reached the distribution level, one of the angels who was a fan of her movies, came with a best idea to place her as the head of the "cost-analysis" court. At first Oscar didn't want not just this position but also the nickname which was given to her. She would argue that this was a man's name and couldn't be hers and she didn't get anything in the court system. However, when the angels told her that she would have the power over a big jelly screen and it would be her exclusive right to show not just regular movies, but movies of real lives, she ultimately agreed and with enthusiasm started working at her new position. What's interesting was that she didn't dream about the golden statue anymore. She said that on her level there many more interesting things to do.

"It is very nice to meet you," said Adam. "I couldn't have thought that in the heaven's chancellery there would be a court like this one."

"Oh yes," said Oscar. "When the various levels of heaven's chancellery were created, we didn't exist, Themis thought that she would be the only one to analyze all cases that go through here and make decisions. There was a lot of reorganization and we finally got the chance to have a cost-analysis on our level."

"So you mean analysis are done here in heaven as well?" said Adam, who wasn't surprised by anything that happened here from the beginning of his journey.

"Of course," said Oscar.

Only then Adam noticed that Oscar was also wearing an elegant dress just like Themis, only hers was of a light beige. Even if she was elderly she still looked beautiful.

"If there wasn't any cost-analysis, then there would be chaos in the heaven's chancellery," she continued. "Themis is of course well known with her subject, but in our case, placing facts and details in the right order is very important."

"So you mean you have the right to intervene in any court of heaven's chancellery?" asked Adam.

"Well, not intervene, but making recommendations," corrected Oscar.

Adam raised his eyebrows and said, "You know about cases before they reach other courts."

"Yes of course," she said. "This is our priority. Well, try to guess. Take a seat and I'll show you."

It was the first time for Adam to be in a situation like this. It seemed to him as if he was in a movie theater where he and his new acquaintance were the only viewers. Oscar came closer to the giant jelly screen and touched it with her finger. On the screen an image came up as in a movie.

"Uuumm, okay, okay, what can I show you?" she pondered as the pictures were moving on the screen. "Well, let's go with this one," she said, and an image came up on the screen of a man who was exonerated whom Adam recently met in the distribution level.

"You of course remember that the man told you that he had already received monetary compensation on earth, and now won't able to receive compensation from seventh level?" she said.

"Yes," said Adam.

"Well, Peter has suffered his part on earth, there's no question about that, but the money which he received won't bring him any good. Soon, his nephew will find him. He's a dishonest businessman. Right now he is near bankruptcy and for his business not to crash, he will ask his uncle to place all his money into his business. After a few years, when the business will prosper, he will kick out your new acquaintance because he wouldn't have any knowledge in this matter and he will trust everything to his nephew. In the next ten years, a poor exoneree will be depressed, will drink alcohol, and will end up being a homeless. His last residence place will be near a grocery store on the corner of 9th Avenue and West 14th street where he will die from coldness in the eve before Christmas. Look, this is his picture."

Adam identified in the picture of an old and poor homeless man, his new acquaintance. It was obvious that Adam got very upset by this.

"However," Oscar continued, "if your new friend wouldn't have received monetary compensation, then it was most likely for him to be eligible for compensation from the seventh level."

"What would have been the compensation?" asked Adam

"Well, look at it yourself," said Oscar and again started moving the pictures on the jelly screen with her finger. "After the ex-prisoner came out of prison, he would have joined with a non-profit organization which helps exonorees to return to life after a couple of years. He would have found out about a secret which his first love didn't tell him for many years. His first love was his classmate with whom he had sex after the prom, got pregnant and gave birth to a son. She then moved to another state and couldn't decide whether to tell him that he had a child. Then she was embarrassed to tell her son that his father was in prison. And only after a few years she would have decided to tell him the truth and he would have met his son. Actually, his son is a great, young man. Their meeting would have been very important and necessary for both of them. After that they would've had a stimuli to live in order to help each other."

Adam looked at the screen and saw two happy faces of a father and son, who lively talked about something. But then, the image disappeared and Oscar said, "However, this meeting will never take place."

So, he doesn't have a chance to be successful?" asked Adam with sad eyes. "May I ask for him, can you review his case instead of mine? No, don't review my case, I don't want it."

"And you're not afraid that your case will not be reviewed, and you will return to earth without anything?" asked the woman strictly looking in Adam's eyes.

"No," said Adam. "I want the father and son to be together."

"Yes, Yes," Oscar was looking at Adam thoughtfully, "The genetics is a strong thing."

Adam couldn't understand what she was saying and asked, "Can I rely on the fact that you will help him?"

"First of all, I'm not the only who decides on that. The only thing I can promise right now is that his case will be sent to the miscarriage of justice court, the 3rd level. They are the ones who did this, let them cleanup their own mess," the woman said with annoyance.

Adam was satisfied with himself that he was trying to help his new friend. And seeing that this woman had empathy towards him, he quietly asked, "Well, what about the two women who were sitting next to me?"

To which Oscar winced at Adam and said, "I know what you mean, Adam, but I won't show you their life story. Everything is quite simple in here. The woman, who was sitting next to you, wants to be abused by her husband. She has many possibilities to leave, but so far, she didn't use any of them. We can't help people if they don't want our help. Regarding the other woman, we already once saved her life. When she tried to get on a bus, at the last second we closed the doors because after two blocks, a bus driver with passengers in the front of the bus died because they hit a refrigerator car. We saved her once. If she in a couple of years won't finish her education and start a new life, her drunken husband will hit her head so hard that she will be taken to the New York Community hospital on Kings Highway in Brooklyn. The doctors will fight for her life for nearly 6 hours, but she will die on the 3rd floor in an intensive care unit and we won't able to save her because we saved her once already.

"So there is no hope for people in cases like these, or any others?" Adam asked with worry.

"Well, there is one last thing that we do for all people when they are near death."

"What is it?" asked Adam "You send them luck?"

"No, it is something much more powerful yet fragile. We send them love," Oscar said softly. "Usually, we give a chance for two people to meet. Sometimes they don't understand what is happening to them. Some of them get scared of these feelings, others get as excited as little children and look very weird, but a few of them do things that scare us. They are killing this feeling inside them without understanding that by doing so, they are killing hope for their future. And not only that, but also they are killing the ability to live their lifetime on earth."

"But what if people can't recognize love the first time? What happens then?" asked Adam.

"Then, there is no other chance at all. We can send them this gift only once in a lifetime, but you have to understand, Adam," she said as she was turning off the screen and moving away from it, "it will be on them how they will properly face love and how they will utilize it to save themselves from death" Oscar finished her speech and it was obvious that she was glancing through the room to see what time it was.

Adam realized that it was time for him to leave. He seemed to be lost in a train of thought and he even was glad that the elevator was stuck on this floor and he got to meet Oscar; because now he started thinking about things that he hadn't thought of before.

As Adam was leaving the big conference room, he thought, "How interesting, every person's life can be watched as a movie. Everything in people's lives is connected; every aspect has a value…"

However, understanding that he had to hurry, he rushed to the elevator because that was his only way to the seventh floor. Even if he pressed 7th button again, the elevator went down because someone called for it. Adam got upset again and thought, "What is it this time?" The doors opened and Adam saw a sign which said "Basement." Two angels came inside the elevator and asked Adam to get out because they had to hurry and take all the boxes upstairs and that he would have to wait for another elevator to come. Adam obediently got off and noticed that the angels started bringing inside elongated boxes on which it said "Careful. Fragile." It was obvious that the boxes were light and the two angels-carriers, were very tender with the boxes. Soon the angels went up in the elevator and while Adam was waiting for another one, he decided to look around.

A couple of workers were walking towards Adam, wearing jumpsuits. He decided to ask them, "What was in the boxes which the angels just took on the elevator?"

"Oh, only one type of boxes are dealt with here," the guys said and laughed at Adam's absence of knowledge. "These were boxes with wings. We manufacture and store all wings here. Then we distribute them by every floor when and if necessary. Look at these," they said and invited him to further, into a room where there were lots of colorful feathers.

"Depending on the individual, we create various wings; they can be of different sizes, big, small, colorful or plain white. It all depends on the person. If the person can fly to big heights then he needs wings with a wide span; and vice versa, if the person doesn't fly high then he needs small wings. We even once had an order for just one wing. Can you believe it, there are people of one wing. Usually they are people who want to fly but don't believe in themselves."

Adam with amazement just took the feathers from the table and started reviewing them and said, "It's the same feathers as I picked up once on the roof, after meeting Ptiscy."

"Speaking of Ptiscy," said one of the workers, "he doesn't have our wings. He was born with them. He comes from a family of angels. His wings are part of his body. We do here special orders for people who are outstanding above other people and give them the chance to fly a little."

"How is that?" Adam asked with surprise.

"Well, yes," they continued, "if the person has the power of will, a dream and desire to do something good for other people, then we usually give them such privilege; to have wings, but temporary and once in a lifetime."

"What a pity," said Adam, then he shook the angels' hands and moved towards the elevator as he noticed that the arrow above the door showed that the elevator was reaching the basement.

"Oh finally," said Adam. He pressed 7th button one more time. The elevator slowly was moving up. He was worried something else might stop him from reaching that floor. But nothing happened, the elevator reached the 7th floor and Adam saw that he had finally reached his destination.

Chapter Eight

The Threshold of Seventh Level of Heaven's Chancellery

On the 7th floor it was very crowded; however, people were dressed very unusually to Adam. It even seemed as if he had entered a costume-party where people would wear costumes of various centuries. A knight with a shining armor passed by almost stepping on his foot, but he didn't even apologize. His helmet was too big for him, and it fell over his eyes and the knight grumbled to himself about it. Then in the corner of a long hall, Adam saw a bald man with a white beard who wore a robe; he was saying something with such deep thought to a group of young people who were surrounding him and listening with amazement on their faces. For a moment, Adam realized that the man was probably Socrates with his group of students. At the other end of the hallway, a couple of men were standing in military uniforms and when he saw the red stars on their uniforms, Adam realized that they were probably Soviet officers. A couple of ladies came up to the officers, who were dressed so beautifully that it seemed as if they had come to a ball, and they had fans in their hands and flowers in their hair, and it seemed as if they were flirting with the officers. In the hall, there were also a few other people walking back and forth wearing costumes, and Adam didn't know to which century or country they belonged. Some of them held various object and Adam was only able to figure out one, which was a man who came up to him holding a light bulb and even though he was wearing a business suit, he still looked odd because his hair was disheveled and he said, "Let me introduce myself, I am Nicola Tesla and this is my invention," and handed Adam a light bulb.

Adam took the light bulb, twirled it in his hands and gave it back to the man thinking that the last thing he needed was a light bulb. Then another man came up to him holding a little treasure box. He was elegantly dressed, wearing a very tight suit and Adam thought, "Oh, another European!"

The man extended his hand and said, "Oh, it's nice to see you, Adam. You must not recognize me, I am Monte Cristo, Count Monte Cristo."

Adam was not surprised that Monte Cristo knew him. It was odd to see that Monte Cristo existed. He didn't want to offend his new acquaintance, and so he asked, "Oh, characters from a book can also ask for compensation in heaven's chancellery?"

Monte Cristo didn't get offended and said, "Well, not all of them. Only the most influential literary characters can turn into real people. The love of people was so powerful that it made me real."

"Oh, what do you have in there, in that box?" asked Adam.

"Before there were various precious stones, but now there are souls of innocent prisoners who were wrongly condemned and they have sent in so many petitions to the earth's courts for their cases to be reviewed, but because no one listened to them, they hardened and from time to time turned into precious stones, and I am their bearer."

Adam went to the end of the hall, and saw a door again with no door knob. As he came closer to the door, one of the officers stood in front of Adam and said, "You know that there is a line here? All of us want our cases to be heard on trial just as much as you do." The officer rudely pointed his finger at the end of the hall where the line ended.

Adam's eyes widened as he exclaimed, "Oh, here, in heaven's chancellery I again have to wait in an endless line, just like in earth's courts?"

At this moment, the door opened and twin sisters came out. They wore a white dress with black polka dots—one dress on the two of them—and when Adam got closer he saw that they were Siamese twins. They looked up on Adam and said in one voice, "Don't listen to this intrusive ghost; he's been coming here since World War II, even though his moral damage was compensated for a long time ago."

"Oh, well, I guess the officer wasn't satisfied with his compensation then."

"On the contrary, he was satisfied; it's just that he had a post-traumatic stress disorder after the war and now even as a ghost, he still has it. I guess it stays within your soul. You can go inside the courtroom now and the bailiff will show you your seat."

"What about the line?" Adam asked.

"There is no line. You are the only one who is scheduled for a hearing."

Adam surprisingly pointed on the line in the hallway and said, "What about the people who are waiting for a hearing?"

"Oh, you must be very sensitive and that's why you can see ghosts."

"Who?" surprisingly said Adam as he raised his eyebrows.

"All the people who you saw in the hall are the souls of people who during many centuries received moral damage. Their cases were already heard, but for some reason they still come here. Probably, your moral damage was so strong that it sharpened your soul and you began seeing ghosts. Well, it's just another proof that you were brought here for a reason."

Adam wanted to see the ghosts in the hallway again, but the door was already closed and no matter how he touched it, it didn't open. The twin sisters said, "There is no way out, your exit will be decided by the court."

Adam turned and went inside the courtroom in order to find his seat. The court wasn't a huge room, and even if there were no elements as in earthly courts, it was obvious that this was a court. Adam was surprised that in the windows and on the floor there were beautiful potted plants; he had never seen potted plants in any earthly court. There were seats made out of marble, benches made out of pink marble and a couple of people sitting there. They gladly waved their hands at Adam as if they had known him for years. In front of the marble benches and seats, there was a marble table in the center of the room, with three chairs. One chair was higher than the others and Adam thought that they must be the seats for the judge and his two advisors. On the left side of the judge's table was a smaller table with two linked chairs and Adam thought that it was probably the place for the secretary, but he was surprised as to why there were two chairs. He realized that the twin sisters were the secretaries. On the right side of the judge's table there was a screen panel and it was also made of jelly, the same as Ptiscy had. In the center of the room, in front of the judge's table, on the floor, there were two circle platforms made out of a darker marble than the floor, one bigger than the other. Adam could not understand why they were needed. Then, beyond the platforms was a marble table and a chair, which was also odd to have in the courtroom. It was placed right in the center between the table for Adam and the prosecutor.

Even though the bailiff was an old and moody man in his 50's with a huge nose like a plum, and showed him to his seat, Adam didn't want to sit in one place and he really wanted to talk to someone. That was why he started walking around the courtroom. He sat next to two old ladies who were chattering nonstop. Their figures were truly unattractive and even though they were seniors, they wore huge, fake jewelry. Every time they were gossiping with excitement and would move their bodies, their jewelry would make noises, they seemed funny to Adam and he imagined them as two old jewelry boxes. He sat closer to them and started asking about the people who would come to the courtroom more and more.

"Would you please tell me who is that tall man in a mantle who just came into the courtroom? He looks very worried," asked Adam.

"Oh, well, that's Ipsos,"[1] said one of the Granny-Boxes. "He was recently moved to our floor. That is, only two or three centuries ago, I don't really remember,"

"I remember," said another Granny-Box who was larger than the other; "he was moved only three centuries ago. Before he was working on the sixth floor and was conducting trials for criminal cases and now he is really unhappy about his promotion."

"Well, I know why," said the smaller Granny-Box. "It's because he is scared of heights, he has acrophobia, only he keeps it a secret."

"Oh, well, now I understand," her friend said. "On the sixth floor the courtroom is narrow with walls and windows which have bars on them, and as you see here everything is very open because we need an exit to a universe."

"My friend's mother's sister's neighbor as we were having tea once told me that Ipsos was once a civil rights activist and was very successful at it. One day at one of their meetings, he was so excited about it that he volunteered to go up on the 9th floor of a building to put up their banner. But he wasn't careful and slipped and fell."

"Oh yes," said a bigger Granny-Box. "This neighbor's cousin's grandfather's co-worker while we were having coffee told me that from that time Ipsos now has claustrophobia."

"Yes, people say that Ipsos clutches his chest every day when the elevator goes up to the seventh floor," said another Granny-Box.

At this point Adam heard a man from the back row say, "Don't listen to these old grannies; they don't know what they are talking about. What awkward people, they come here every day as if they were invited," said the old man.

Adam came up to him and asked, "And you were invited here?"

"Yes," the old man answered and took out an easel and brushes. "I am a cartoonist, and I will be drawing portraits of all the court participants, including you."

Adam liked the cartoonist and he sat next to him.

"Why does the court have such unusual secretaries?" Adam asked

"Why unusual? All secretaries in the court, ever since the creation of the world, have been Siamese twins. They were necessary," the cartoonist explained.

"Why two? Why is it important?" asked Adam.

"Well, they are writing the court transcript and the transcript always has to be twofold."

"Sorry, but I still don't understand. Why twofold?

"Well, every side in the transcript will see what they want to see. The lawyer will see all the information he needs in the transcript in order to prove his client's innocence. The prosecutor in the transcript will see all the information needed to prove the guilt of the person that is being tried. That's why the transcript is always written by the twins Vivimas[2] who but they would know better about it."

"Why would they know better?" Adam asked with curiosity.

"Well, because once twins Vivimas were born on earth as Siamese twins. Since they have one body for two, they were given only one birth certificate and one name for the two of them; however, their personalities are very opposite. That's why when they came here, they were the ones who influenced a new policy in the heaven's chancellery, which is to have a two-fold court transcript.

"Oh," Adam nodded his head as if he understood what the cartoonist told him, but truly he still didn't understand anything.

Adam looked at the cartoonist's things and saw a portrait book.

"Is that where you'll be drawing the court participants and me?"

"Yes, I have been a cartoonist for many centuries. Would you like to look at the portraits I have done so far?"

The cartoonist handed Adam his easel, and Adam started looking through various portraits. He saw a portrait of Nicola Tesla and Monte Cristo and even Socrates. But then he saw a portrait of a man that looked very familiar to him. In a moment, he realized that the man was his grandfather Nicholas, the very one who inspired him to choose his profession.

"I really like your portraits. They look very realistic. You must have been born with this talent." Adam said.

The Cartoonist just laughed in return and said, "Oh Adam, I was no artist when I was alive, that's for sure. I used to be a palm reader, a profession that I hope no one will come across in their lives."

"Palm reader? Oh, then you can predict people's fate by the lines on their palms," said Adam.

"Honestly, this is a questionable field of study. Sometimes messengers would come to me and warn me that I shouldn't play with people's minds like that. However, I liked this profession and I would boast that I can identify a person just by his/her palm. But as you see I was wrong. After I came here, I was sentenced to work here as a cartoonist so that I could observe people's faces because that's the most important feature of a person."

Adam only looked at him and wouldn't say anything in order not to look narrow-minded. So, he just nodded his head from time to time. The Cartoonist continued his story and said, "In our court, everything is quite different from earthly courts. People here don't believe in palm readings, DNA, fingerprints, and other standard types of evidence. You'll see that for yourself very soon, Adam." concluded the Cartoonist.

Adam saw that a man was coming towards him and the cartoonist whispered to him, "He is coming for you."

Adam stood momentarily and looked at the man in a cape who had very intelligent elongated features; he was very tall and even his fingers were long; he looked like a golfer and Adam thought that the man was probably British.

"My name is Coeus[3] and I will be your attorney for this trial," said the man who sounded British.

"But I don't have the means to pay for an attorney," Adam said apologetically.

"My dear Adam, on the earth you people have two options: you either pay big money for a fancy attorney in order to get something similar to justice; or you have a free attorney who either only knows his first ABCs of the law or has no interest in defense at all. Honestly, both of these options are absurd, because one of them worries about prestige and money and the others just doing this job because there was an open position," Coeus pointed at and waved to someone coming into the court. Adam, however, noticed the doors to the court weren't opening at all. People would just appear as if out of thin air.

"Anyway, in both cases, this is not what justice is all about. Oh, I remember recently, in our court's newsletter, there was an article about an earthly court where one of the free attorneys forced his client to plea bargain and state that he is guilty only because he was overwhelmed with cases that month and didn't have time to check the subject matter of this case. We sometimes look at these free attorneys who come to the hearing either drunk or sleepy, and always complain that because they are not paid enough at their jobs, they shouldn't bother working hard. That's why we recently had a meeting and we decided that people who were wrongfully convicted because of such free attorneys, should have their cases reviewed here immediately. And plus, here on the 7th floor we believe that justice cannot be measured and bought with money. Here money is just dirty garbage." He patted Adam's shoulder and continued, "Let's take a walk, my friend. How was your ride here?"

"Fine, thank you. I was brought here by Phaeton," Adam answered.

"Oh, that's just marvelous. It's a good thing that they didn't send a Pegasus for your pick up. They can be very frisky; they are always stopped by STEP, the sky traffic enforcement patrol, which then sends us tickets for their violations. And you know what's funny, Pegasus always denies that he has violated the flying rules," said Coeus.

Adam started laughing and Coeus continued, "Yesterday, one of my friends, who is an attorney from the fifth floor who deals with trials related with family cases, told me that one young Pegasus brought in a plaintiff, though he was so nauseated that the court session had to wait for the plaintiff to finish throwing up," laughed Coeus. "By the way, who was the coachman that brought you here on the Phaeton?"

"Amaxas," answered Adam.

"Oh, my old friend Max. You know he has a significant stability in any environment, on earth or in heaven, and he will always be a coachman. For many years he worked at New York's Central Park as a coachman and brought cheer to many families on weekends. That's why through many resumes when we were looking for a person on an open position for a coachman, we decided to choose him as our candidate. Stability on both earth and in heaven is a very important aspect, my friend. You'll learn about that later, Adam."

Adam was surprised by how Coeus was calm before the trial. Then Adam got very worried as to why his attorney was talking about some nonsense and not about the hearing that was about to start. It seemed as if the attorney read Adam's thoughts, as he turned to him and said, "Don't worry, my dear friend Adam. I am a good counsel, though I never advertise myself. Today I am scheduled for a hearing of your case in this courtroom, and this means that throughout the whole hearing, I will be by your side. It's not like in an earthly court when the lawyer tries to manage to present various cases in different courtrooms, all in one day, and so they end up sweating and wearing out their shoes just to get more money."

Adam was surprised and remarked, "I am impressed by your knowledge about the counsels on earth. But may I ask how you know such dreary truths about them? It must be because your previous clients from earth have complained to you about them?"

To which Coeus smiled and calmly explained, "No, Adam, I didn't just hear the dreary truths from my previous clients, I also get to witness it from time to time."

"How come?" Adam asked.

"Well, technically I am not just a counsel in heaven's chancellery, I also have a mission: I am an archangel.

"An archangel?" Adam asked. "But how is that related to the courts?"

"Oh, let me explain everything to you from the beginning," said Coeus, and walked to the corner of the courtroom with Adam.

"Many many long years ago, I used to work as an archivist at the State Supreme Court of New York. I worked in a very small room in the basement and because it was cold there, I was always sick and was coughing non-stop. And believe me, I looked very different from what I look like now. I used to be a small, hunched bald old man with bad eyesight and wore glasses as big and thick as loops. The same way my flower pots looked. I tried to take care of them by placing them closer to the sun but they always withered. I received a very small salary, but I loved this job because I liked reading all the cases which went through our court, and believe me I had my knowledge for these cases. One day, while looking at one of the folders that recently came in, I saw the defendant's name, and he happened to be my childhood friend and I saw that he was most likely to be sentenced to the death penalty. I started looking more thoroughly into the case and saw that there was no real evidence that would link my friend to the crime. Also his petition for another expertise was denied and his counsel didn't file a claim either. Then, in the case transcript I saw a lot of mistakes and errors, and I was really worried about my friend and wanted to help him any way possible. I was trying to see him in jail, but I wasn't allowed. I got a letter from him which had only one phrase: "*I am innocent, believe me.*" After that, I tried to contact the judge, the prosecutor and even his counsel, but no one listened to me. When I was pointing to a few mistakes, the judge laughed at me and said, "How can you know things about jurisprudence? You're not a lawyer; your place is in the archive, go and work there. You have no business here." Years passed and I couldn't prove anything, and my friend was executed. I was very depressed and worried that I hadn't been able to do anything for him. A few days after his execution, I had a heart attack while I was sitting at work, by my desk and my head fell on an open folder with his case."

Coeus went silent for a moment, and Adam saw that it was hard for Coeus to again remember that moment in his life. Adam wanted to ask Coeus not to go on with his painful story, but Coeus had already resumed his story, "However, I was pleasantly surprised when after my death, I followed the light at the end of the tunnel, and two angels met me and told me that I would continue working in the court. They showed me the heaven's chancellery building. I tried looking for a place where the archive was located, however the angel who led me, said, "Oh, Coeus you will be working as a lawyer from now on. We believe you have enough qualities to represent the cases from earth in the heaven's chancellery," and that's how I got a new identity and became an elegant gentleman," concluded Coeus.

"And what happened with your friend's case?" Adam asked.

To which Coeus answered, "Oh, I was right about Archio[4] being innocent and the court making numerous mistakes. In the 70's of the last century, when DNA evidence became popular in earthly courts, my friend's case was reviewed again and it was concluded he was wrongfully convicted. I saw him a few times here, and through my recommendations, he is now working as an archivist in the heaven's chancellery. And can you believe it, he, as I did many years ago, is reading cases and is trying to find mistakes in our court process. So far, no luck." Coeus laughed.

Adam laughed too, and stopped worrying about his upcoming hearing. After which Coeus continued and said, "That's why, my friend Adam, as an archangel I have the privilege of going back and forth between earth and heaven."

"What about other representative of the heaven's chancellery such as Ptiscy, Angela Phoros, Max …" Adam began saying

To which Coeus pointed out, "Oh, yes, I don't just jump up and down between heaven and earth, I can also intervene in people's lives by changing the course of events", Coeus explained.

"By the way, in heaven's chancellery I still haven't seen the angels who came to me the first time"

"Oh they are all doing well, except for Ptiscy," said Coeus. "You remember he was arrested on earth when he got stuck on a tree in Central Park. Kumbi was very upset with him because this was not his first time getting in trouble. Before, due to his way of walking, he had police be reasonably suspicious of him. As you say on earth, he was stopped and frisked," Coeus laughed a little. "But thankfully he was released. Honestly, we have gotten tired of dealing with his troubles and erasing memories of people and his criminal records."

"So he was fired from his job as a messenger?" asked Adam.

"Not at all, Kumbi is a fair judge and that's why he sent Ptiscy to an extra workshop for a flying technique. He will get extra lessons for a while, and after he passes his flying test, he will able to return to his job as a messenger." Coeus explained.

"Oh, poor Ptiscy," said Adam. "He was the first one of you guys who I met."

Coeus continued to calmly walk around the courtroom, and then he came up to the flower pots, took one of them and placed it on the other window. This seemed odd to Adam, since the sun was shining everywhere, equally. Coeus continued, "As you see, my dear Adam, in heaven's chancellery, the court process is so precise, you can't even imagine it. There are no mistakes in the transcripts, all the court participants come to the hearing on time, and there is no way to forge or steal the evidence, and no one can bribe the judge or the prosecutor, and no one is able to scare the witnesses and, most importantly, everybody here is telling only the truth. You'll see how."

NOTES

1. IPSOS—from the Greek, meaning height.
2. VIVIMAS—from the Greek meaning twins.
3. COEUS—in Greek mythology the god of intelligence.
4. ARCHIO—from the Greek, means archive.

Chapter Nine

Heaven's Chancellery

The Trial Begins

Adam heard someone say from nowhere in a commanding manner, "The trial is beginning!"

"Everybody, take your seats," the voice continued.

Adam hurried to his seat next to Coeus. It seemed very funny to Adam how Vivimas tried to sit down on two chairs at one time but couldn't since their right legs were getting twisted. It seemed that the courtroom got crowded in a second even though the door through which he entered didn't open. The people in the crowd were strangers to Adam and he couldn't figure why so many people were in the courtroom right when the hearing was about to start. In the place where a prosecutor usually sits, there was Ipsos; he looked very pale and was constantly looking around at everybody somewhat fearfully. Granny-Boxes were all around him as he was placing his right hand on the left side of his chest. He wore a royal blue cape and a velvet cap with a tassel. Adam thought that Ipsos looked like a PhD graduate from law school who hadn't got any job offers yet and was actively looking for one, instead of a prosecutor.

Adam noticed that out of nowhere a young lady appeared in the courtroom who was so beautiful and effulgent that the whole crowd hushed as she came towards them. It was obvious that Coeus had liked her for a while because as she was walking in, he tried to camouflage his feelings and quietly whispered to Adam, "This is Arianna,[1] and she will offer expertise of emotions."

"Why emotions?" quietly asked Adam.

"There is no other way, because you can fake the evidence, but you can never fake your emotions. Through emotions it is easier to find out the truth within the person. But you'll see everything yourself very soon."

Arianna passed near them and the train from her cloak lightly touched their shoulders. A scent of spring rain was coming from her and Adam noticed that she had the most beautiful and unusual cloak in the courtroom; it was shimmering with different colors and her hair was of golden locks. In Adam's head, her image did not stick with the idea that she would be the one offering expertise.

As if hearing what Adam was thinking, Coeus quietly whispered to Adam. "You're right she doesn't look like an expert. Before, Arianna was a professional diver and the colors which she uses during her expertize she saw when she would go under the depths of the ocean. She once told me that such indescribable, beautiful colors which she saw under the ocean, you can never see even in heaven. Diving under the ocean and seeing these colors gives you such truthful emotions which you can't fake them on earth."

Adam wanted to ask Coeus why she stood on a marble platform in the center of the courtroom and did not take a seat in one of the chairs of the court participants, but he didn't ask any more questions in order not to look empty-headed.

In a couple of minutes, from beneath the courtroom, the silhouette of a man appeared; he was in his sixties, not tall, but stocky, and even though by the way he walked, it was obvious that he was very aware of what he was doing and that he was always right, he was still nervously patting his cloak, just above his belly, as if he was looking for a button. He wore a dark purple cloak with golden stripes and had on a velvet cap. He wasn't alone; he was escorted by two ladies. The woman who was walking on his left side looked very weird; she was either crying or laughing. The woman who was walking by his right side was, on the contrary, very quiet, calm and emotionless. All of them were heading towards the table where usually the judges sat. Adam looked around and saw that all the court participants including himself took their seats and he figured that probably at any moment now, something very important was about to begin.

However, the hearing did not start and Adam finally asked Coeus, "Are we waiting for someone to come?"

Coeus raised his eyebrows and said, "We are waiting for Themis. No court on any level is going to take place unless Themis joins the trial. By the way, one of the reasons to make a plea for a mistrial and for the case to be heard again is if Themis was not present. But in my practice, this has never happened."

"Oh, I've met her before. She's a very beautiful woman—and have you seen how naturally gorgeous her body is, especially her…? Anyway, she assured me that she would come to my hearing."

Coeus, darkly smiled and said, "Look, I don't think you should have hopes about you two."

Adam turned away from Coeus, as he didn't want to look Coeus in the eye, and instead he just looked down at his shoes. Coeus, however, did not hesitate and continued, "Well, maybe you have a little chance with her because you are not a lawyer. Folks from my department said that no lawyer could steal her heart since she doesn't like lawyers, who take money and promise to give justice." Adam smiled a little and Coeus continued, "You know her very first lover was a scientist, just like you. I heard that he created a very useful invention for mankind, I just don't remember which one though."

Adam saw how the door from which he entered opened and Themis came in.

"Oh, look, look, she's coming," Adam whispered to Coeus, trying to shut him up, so Themis wouldn't hear them.

It seemed that this time Themis looked even more beautiful. She had changed her dress and this time she was wearing a loose-fitting white dress with violet irises. Her hair was accessorized by a purplish blue scarf. But what caught Adam's eyes were her earrings. She was wearing tanzanite-cut dangle earrings which were completing her look. As she walked along, everybody who was present in the room was looking at her with astonishment. By her face, it was obvious that she liked that everybody was overwhelmed by her beauty. She walked straight ahead toward the judge's table, but then she stopped and turned to Adam. Adam liked the feeling that from everybody who was present in the courtroom, she decided to come up to him. He remembered Coeus speaking about her and said, "This dress suits you very well and those earrings look perfect on you as well. You have good taste in picking that color."

"Oh, thank you. I am well aware that you are one of the best experts in precious stones. And thank you for noticing my dress, I designed it myself," she said blushing.

After which, Themis left Adam and took her honorable place, which was somewhat near to him. She was sitting in the center of the courtroom just before the two marble circle platforms. At one point she announced, "Let the trial of Adam's Compensation for Moral Damage begin!"

Her voice echoed throughout the courtroom and everybody including Adam felt a breeze coming out of nowhere.

NOTE

1. ARIANNA—in Greek mythology, the goddess of colors and emotions.

Chapter Ten

Heaven's Chancellery

The Trial

The Judge began to speak and Adam finally heard his voice, "Today we are gathered here in Heaven's chancellery on 06/13/2007 to review Adam's case for compensation for moral damage caused by *Only the Truth* newspaper and the article's writer, Mr. Lampoon[1] and also by the chairman of the Department of Earth Science at the New York University of Geology, Mr. Ali Baster. Today we have a full court under the seventh level of Heaven's Chancellery, Judge Kumbi,[2] me, my right assistant Mello,[3] who will help me be right-minded, and my left assistant Synaisthema,[4] who will help me be sensitive."

After which, Kumbi nodded to Coeus and said, "For the opening statement, Coeus, the counsel for the plaintiff, is invited to the marble stand."

Coeus went up to the marble circle platforms and Adam was surprised that Coeus stood on the smaller platform and that he didn't have any folders or papers as any other things that lawyers would usually have. Adam even got scared that Coeus wouldn't remember all the names and dates or the facts that were needed for the case. However, Coeus began his speech with a very confident and calm voice, and from his first sentences it was obvious that he knew everything about Adam's life. However, when he looked around, he realized that Coeus' knowledge was the least shocking factor; first and foremost, Adam was presently sitting on a marble chair in Heaven's Chancellery, where he was brought by the Phaeton. Coeus for a second looked at Adam as if he had read his thoughts, raised his eyebrows, sneered for a moment and continued his speech to the judges and the audience.

"As Adam's counsel, I know everything about Adam's life. First I would like to begin with the fact that my client has been affected by a tremendous moral damage for a period of time and the cause of that is because Adam has been working on an invention for about 10 years, which will most likely bring benefits to the people in the world. Adam has two significant degrees; he has a Master's in Geology and he is a medical doctor. These two specializations Adam chose not by chance, as his grandfather, Nicholas, who was a very experienced surgeon from Russia, was the one who inspired him to choose his professions and continue working on an invention which his grandfather started. Over ten years, Adam conducted research at the Geology Institute in which he elicited the healing properties of various precious stones. For such matter, he developed his grandfather's invention further, so that it would be beneficial in the present time. At the beginning of his research, the chairman of the Geology Department, Ali Baster, noticed that Adam's research had potential and so he decided to morally crush Adam and have him rethink his invention's value. However, Adam didn't hesitate and continued his research and often worked after-hours in the laboratory, and as a result he published a monograph about the healing properties of some precious stones and how they can be used for medical purposes. Ali Baster became afraid that Adam's invention would be popular…"

"Objection, your honor!" exclaimed the prosecutor, Ipsos; "we cannot conclude whether Adam's invention will be popular and beneficial around the world, and there is no evidence for such a matter; that's why I make a plea to dismiss this charge against Mr. Ali Baster."

"We do have a witness for such a matter, and we will question him later," stated Coeus.

"Sustained," exclaimed Kumbi and he nodded at Coeus.

Adam began to sort out all the people who would able to prove that, but he couldn't think of anyone. Meanwhile Coeus continued, "As I was saying, Mr. Ali Baster became afraid that Adam would be more successful than him and that his subordinate would turn out to be smarter and wealthier. That's why he paid a journalist, Mr. Lampoon, to write series of articles criticizing Adam's invention. At the restaurant called Gethsemane Garden, Mr. Lampoon received various pieces of information from Ali Baster about certain weak points in Adam's research, as well as a bribe in the amount of $3,000 which here is equivalent to 30 silver coins."

After such words, a sigh echoed through the audience and Coeus understood the uproar and so held a moment of silence for them to return from their train of thoughts. Then, Coeus continued, "When the articles by Mr. Lampoon began to be published one after the other, Adam got very depressed and worried very much. Ali Baster hypocritically felt sorry for Adam and tried to better get to know his findings that were not discussed in the monograph. Finally, one night, Ali Baster sneaked into Adam's laboratory, stole separate parts of Adam's invention, journals, graphs, and finally, set the laboratory on fire and left the scene. Adam was accused of having an accidental fire, he was fired from his job, and had to pay a debt for damages. After some time, Mr. Ali Baster published his own monograph and made a presentation of 'his' invention. The same journalist, Mr. Lampoon, later wrote a series of articles in which he praised Mr. Ali Baster's invention."

Ipsos interrupted, "Your Honor, I would like to clarify some points. Today we are reviewing compensation for moral damage which is under the umbrella of the civil court. Why then does the counsel of the plaintiff impose on Mr. Ali Baster and Mr. Lampoon criminal sanctions?" Ipsos smirked and looked at Coeus, then continued, "If you have enough evidence to prove the arson, bribery, slander, then I suggest you open a criminal lawsuit and go a floor down."

To which Coeus answered, "As you may know, dear Ipsos, I never specialized in criminal cases and right now as I was explaining the subject matter, I just mentioned that such crimes had occurred which led to my client's moral damage."

It was obvious that Ipsos sat crushed and was shaking his head irritably. Meanwhile Coeus continued, "In regards to evidence, here on the 7th floor, everything is quite different. In regards to arson, Ali Baster has an aura that looks like a huge fire that will be with him for the rest of his life. In regards to the bribery, both Mr. Ali Baster's and Mr. Lampoon's hands will have a green aura for the rest of their lives. Arianna has easily proved that, but I don't want to focus on it, because I strongly believe that the moral damage is harsher and much more hurtful than any other type of damage."

Coeus was satisfied with his answer and continued his speech, "At first, Adam tried to talk to Mr. Ali Baster and hoped that it was just a mistake, but Ali Baster didn't even talk to him. Adam was hurt day by day when he saw that the whole world got to know about his invention and at the same time was named after Ali Baster. Adam lost all hope and decided to file a lawsuit in the district civil court regarding the compensation for moral damage against Mr. Ali Baster and against the journalist Mr. Lampoon and to restore his authorship of the invention. The trial went on for many years and after Adam couldn't provide enough evidence and paid way too much money for attorneys, he lost the case. This is not surprising, as most of his time Adam was at the laboratory and all the evidence that would have helped was destroyed in the fire, and that's why he couldn't prove the plagiarism. His grandfather Nicholas, who inspired him to do this research and had the original data, at that time had joined us in heaven. That's why Adam didn't have a chance. Adam took all his money that was left and gave it to the lawyer to appeal the case; however, the appeal trial which took many years was lost. In the present time, the Supreme Court has decided to review the petition to the same court; Adam has also signed a petition through Ptiscy."

After Coeus' speech, suddenly a sobbing cry came from Kumbi's left side advisor, Synaisthema. While the right advisor, Mello, was very calm and seemed to be in a train of thought. Kumbi looked at both of them, then at Ipsos and said, "Do you have anything to add?"

"No, your honor," said Ipsos.

"Since the prosecutor doesn't have anything to add, let's call the witnesses."

Coeus stood up and said, "Your honor, I would like to first question Adam's grandfather Nicholas, but he is under the supervision of another temple, and that's why I need special permission from Themis."

All this time, Themis was sitting quietly in her seat, and just nodded to Coeus. At the same time, the door through which Adam entered opened and Adam's grandfather walked in. He strode confidently and stood on the small marble platform while Arianna was standing near on the big one. Adam wasn't surprised that he saw his grandfather in this court since it seemed that anything was possible here. He was surprised, however, that his grandfather looked younger than the age at which he died. Adam really wanted to run up and hug his grandfather as he used to do when he was little, sit on his lap and breathe in his smell. But he was quietly sitting next to Coeus and didn't want to disobey the court ordinance.

"Witness Nicholas," Kumbi said, "do you understand why you are present in this court?"

"Yes," Adam's grandfather said calmly, "in order to help review the case of my grandson Adam."

"Are you allowing Arianna to offer an expertise of your aura?" asked Kumbi

"Yes, I am allowing it," Nicholas answered.

"Counsel, you may begin your questioning," said Kumbi, nodding towards Coeus.

At the same moment, Ipsos quickly got up and exclaimed, "Objection! Objection, your honor! We cannot question Nicholas as a witness since the case regarding his compensation for moral damage was already reviewed only a century ago."

Kumbi asked secretaries Vivimas, "Please get the folder Ipsos is referring to."

Both secretaries stood at once and at the same time with their pointing fingers started to draw a jelly screen in the air. Adam saw the jelly screen was the same as Ptiscy's. Vivimas started flipping through the pages on the screen and found case #010328 of 1954, Nicholas v. KGB. Then, Vivimas lightly pushed the jelly screen towards the judge and he caught it.

"Thank you, secretaries. You may take your seats," said Kumbi.

He took a quick look at the case and continued, "Oh, yes, I remember this case. Right after World War II, a lot of cases were reviewed here at that time. This case solution satisfied the plaintiff's side," said Kumbi.

"Our side doesn't question the fact that Nicholas has been here before. We are respecting all the laws and we do not question the "one–time appearance" rule. According to which, a person may only be in the court only once in a life time. However, referring to the case Anthropos[5] v. Kako[6] any court participant is allowed to be in this court a second time and be questioned only if his permanent residence became Heaven."

"Sustained," said Kumbi, and he nodded at Coeus so that he would continue.

The prosecutor shook his head and frowned. He put his hand on his chest and it was obvious that he began to feel even worse, while Coeus continued questioning Nicholas.

"Please tell us, Nicholas, which moral damage have you faced and why?" asked Coeus.

"Well, it all began in the beginning of 1945, at the end of World War II. Back then I was working as a navy surgeon in a hospital. This period was especially tough because more and more injured soldiers and officers were brought from the battlefield while the medications for their treatment were scarce. Then, it came to mind that there were some precious stones which had healing properties and might help the soldiers."

"But where did you find these precious stones while you were in the hospital and during the war?" Coeus asked with surprise.

"Well, we can call this a lucky circumstance. In our hospital a young woman was working as a doctor. One day in the locker room I saw that she was hiding something in her white robe. I wanted to warn her that if she had something illegal or stolen then everybody would have problems with the administration. But she calmed me down and said that it was only a jewelry box with precious stones which her family had had for generations. The problem was that this young doctor was from a Russian noble family back in the day and it was destroyed by the Communists after the Revolution of 1917. She was afraid that she was going to get killed as well and that's why she made up her new origins and would say that her family were peasants. She pled with me to keep her secret and I did. Then, it came to my mind to ask her if we could use these precious stones for treating the soldiers, and she agreed. Since there were a lot of injured soldiers sent to the hospital, my colleagues and I were very worried about them and brainstormed in order to create something that would help the soldiers. Then, I remember how one night I constructed a little machine made out of quartz loop and other instruments which I had on hand. The machine would direct a beam of light towards a precious stone and at the injuries. One of my colleagues, Ivan, got a cold and was getting only worse and we couldn't help him and the only thing I could suggest is to try out the machine. Since this was his only choice, he agreed. By the end of the day, the doctor felt a lot better. The fever was gone and it was easier for him to breathe. After that, it was decided to use the machine on soldiers."

"And what were the results of your invention?" asked Coeus with curiosity on his face. It was obvious that other members of the court and the audience were all curious to find out the results. Everybody wanted to know except for Adam, because he had already heard this story from his grandfather more than once and because he already had seen how this worked.

"The results were significant," Nicholas continued. "Little wounds were healing right before my eyes, and on the big wounds, such procedures had to be done a couple of times. We were able to treat hundreds of soldiers and officers, plus their immune systems got better as well, and many of them began to look younger and some chronic illnesses were treated as well."

"May I clarify which exact precious stones you used? Or did you use one that healed everything?" asked Coeus.

"Not at all. Later my colleagues and I began to see that emeralds and aquamarine helped heal eye injuries. We stopped bleeding by using pearls and alexandrite. Then we realized that rubies fought heart disease, while carnelian healed open injuries. Two significant ones were topaz, which treated tuberculosis, and opal, which healed frostbit limbs. But the most powerful healing power was a diamond because it would help not only heal illnesses but also stabilize mental conditions and even heal paralysis," concluded Nicholas.

"I object. Even when we were reviewing your case the first time, I was already against such an idea. You conducted experiments on people and all this treatment was under the question of whether it helped and to whom specifically," stated Ipsos.

At the same moment Adam stood up and wanted to oppose and say that it was not true, but then he realized that he was in court and he couldn't really oppose what the prosecutor had said, and he quietly sat down. An echo of indignation spread around the audience and it seemed that the Granny-Boxes were turning their heads 180 degrees and the sound of little bells clinking sounded around the courtroom.

"Order, Order," Kumbi screamed at the audience.

In a couple of minutes the audience hushed and Grandfather Nicholas continued his story.

"The same way the KGB and the leaders of the Communist Party reacted was that shortly after, they arrested not only me but my colleagues as well who also had used precious stones for the healing treatment. We were charged with anti-Soviet activities, specifically, harboring precious stones, causing harm to soldiers of Soviet Army, aiding and abetting the Nazi Army and for some reason calling for the overthrow of the Soviet Government. I remember clearly when my colleagues and I were taken into an interrogation room and each of us faced all the KGB brutality for hours. We weren't given any food or water. We weren't allowed to sleep either, so we didn't know whether it was day or night. It was plain torture that felt endless and each of us was thinking why death didn't come sooner. Then, the captain of the police guard came in and brought that young woman whose stones we used for treating the soldiers. It was obvious that she was also beaten numerously times because she was all blue from bruises. Meanwhile the captain had a folder with a red line across it in his hands. He told us, "You all know that you will be given a punishment for the crimes which you have committed. But first, I will tell you why, or rather who is the reason you are being punished."

The guards dragged the young woman to stand close to the captain as he opened the folder and started reading from the papers.

"This woman is not really a peasant as she has been telling you all this time. Her real name is Maria Markovsky and she comes from a noble family. She is a countess. Her family lived in Poland, where they had a castle, which was passed down through the generations. Then the family moved to Russia where they opened several skin-processing factories where they would exploit people and make money. After the Revolution when the Communists took power, their factories and property were given to the government. Her grandfather and father were killed. She and her mother had fake documents and lied to the government and to society that she was a peasant and was able to get a job in a hospital. But as you see the KGB knows everything and that's why we were able to find out her evil plans and stop her in time so that she wouldn't harm Soviet society further. But since you were helping her, you are now her accomplices in crime and therefore should be punished with her. But I have happy news for you. You will receive a less harsh punishment than she and will be sent to Siberian camps. While Maria Markovsky will be executed by a firing squad tonight and her daughter will be sent to an orphanage. Thanks to Stalin, who is very kind to children, no matter who the children come from, he still mandates the government to raise them properly."

"Unfortunately, everything that the captain said was true. The young doctor who was the owner of the precious stones was shot by the firing squad later in the day, while my colleague and I were sent to a super-maximum security correction camp in Siberia for 20 years," concluded Nicholas.

"What happened with your invention and the precious stones?" asked Coeus.

"They were confiscated the first day of our arrest by the representative of the KGB. By the way, while interrogating us, they asked me to draw how my machine worked and I thought that they were planning to further analyze it themselves in the Soviet laboratories. But you have to understand that all inventions which were very important and significant had to be under the control of the government and the authorship of all inventions could be finalized only by the government. Anyway, when we reached Siberia, the climate was hard getting used to. The weather was always freezing while we had to cut down trees for 12 hours a day without a proper diet or warm clothing. From such a tough environment a dozen prisoners were dying each day. They would be taken away like logs and buried all together. All the prisoners were abused, tired, hungry and cold; they would fight with each other every day for a crumb of bread. There was nothing humane out there in Siberia. The worst thing is that we had to work with felons who weren't humane, but during such a tough time we were all suffering in the same way and that's why one day both groups of criminals and our intelligent innocent group decided to run away to Norway. In the camp where we lived, there were a few attempts of an escape and prisoners would mostly run away to Finland, which was closer to the border to the camp. Even if their escape was successful, still the Finland government didn't want to ruin their relations with the Soviet Union and would give back those runaway prisoners. These people then faced a much harsher punishment. That's why we decided that the only place we could run is Norway. It was much further, but we hoped that at least some of us would able to reach it and be safe. For a few months, in strict secrecy, we were planning how to escape. But you must understand that we didn't have much equipment or tools; we took a few crumbs of bread, a rope, a box of matches and a small knife. Early in the morning when the patrolmen fell asleep, we caught that moment and jumped over the fence which secured the whole camp. I remember we were running for a while without looking back into the forest because we knew that once the patrolmen found out that we had ran away, their dogs would easily catch our scent. This was one of the scariest sunrises in my life. I remember how it was the first time I didn't want the sun to rise and each of us looked at the sky and prayed for the sun to rise later so that we were not caught by the guards. I remember how we looked on the sky that was beginning to get brighter and each of us prayed to our own God in different languages and even the ones who didn't know any prayers would make up their own. It seemed to me that at that point, time lost its dimension and fear united our group of people into one creature who was running across the taiga and felt only fear, which made us go farther and farther. When the sun rose, we understood that we don't have any energy left to go any further and we needed to stop, make a fire and find food. However, there were no animals to hunt and we saw a group of criminals who were also looking for food. Luckily, our paths separated and for a few days we were wandering around the taiga for a road to Norway's border. This was a harsh feeling to fight with the cold and with hunger because the first days, fear was our drug that kept us moving further and not notice the cold weather or our hunger. We tried to eat tree bark and one day in the tree hollow we found nuts and acorns which must have been hidden by squirrels. That's how we moved further and further, tried to joke around and sing songs, anything that would cheer us up and give us hope that we could get to Norway, where we would get food, clothes and most importantly—freedom. We didn't have any energy left, some of our group members died by falling under the ice when we were crossing a lake. We all had frostbitten toes and fingers, but we still kept on walking. After a few days we saw a horrible picture; we saw an extinguished campfire which was most likely made by the group of criminals. Around it were fragments of bones and parts of a human body, and pieces of ripped clothing. The snow around it was red with blood, and our doubts about the criminal group were right. In the beginning of our escape, we already noticed that the leader of their group decided to take a young prisoner with him and we thought that he planned to be their emergency food for all of them, and that's how it was. But we didn't have anything else to do but to take in that horrible and ugly truth and we continued going farther and promising each other that even if one of us was able to get to Norway, we would definitely tell the truth about the tragedy that we lived through. It seemed that our prayers were heard and next morning we were able to catch a couple of birds and make a meal out of them. In the evening of the same day, on the horizon we saw dark fences and we understood that we were getting closer to people. I remember how we were walking very slowly and were practically crawling our last steps. When we saw a few people moving towards us, we fainted…"

It was obvious that it was hard for Grandfather Nicholas to speak. Vivimas brought him water which he drank, and he took a deep breath. People in the courtroom felt sympathetic, and he continued

"When I woke up, I understood that I was located in some place that looked like a hospital and the first thing I saw was a window with short white curtains and some insect which was beating on the window, trying to get outside. It would fly away and then try to fly right through the window. I would constantly hear a boom-boom-boom, and I thought it was my vein pulsing near my temple. I couldn't feel my arms or legs and when I tried to open my lips in order to ask for water, I heard a crack and after a few minutes I realized that it was my voice which mumbled something that didn't sound like a phrase asking for water. The only thing I could do was to turn my head left and right and then I saw that there were no soldiers in a uniform, no barking dogs or that rotten smell which was all over the camp, and I was at least happy about that. After a few days I got better and I found out that our escape was successful, and my colleague and I had reached Norway and were now receiving treatment. However, out of the 8 people, only two of us survived, my friend Ivan, who was a doctor from our hospital, and I. This was a tough and happy moment in my life. A happy one because after many years, I could finally taste the freedom and safety; but also dreadful because I had to learn how to walk and speak again. I had frostbitten toes and fingers, and my throat was damaged. At that moment I felt as if I was in a fog and I couldn't fully understand that this was reality and a possibility to start a new life and try to forget all the nightmares of my past life. One day when I was talking to my friend, I noticed that his hair was fuller and the grey hair which had been on his temples was darkening. I patted his head to make sure his hair was real,

"Yes, yes, it's true," said Ivan, "and two of my teeth have grown back. And at night," he whispered to Nicholas, "I have a desire for women." They both looked at each other with astonished eyes.

"So it's true then," Nicholas said breaking the silence, "what the soldiers were saying, after using the diamond in the machine. Remember, they said they not only healed but also got younger."

"Yes," said Ivan. "I did the right thing agreeing to that experiment. And you, Nicholas, were dumb for not agreeing. You would have been as young as me."

Nicholas just sadly smiled at Ivan and said, "Well, it wasn't my faith then. As we say in Russia, I'm the shoemaker without shoes."

Coeus didn't want to interrupt Nicholas' story, but he asked him, "What happened with the group of criminals. Were any of them able to survive?"

"No, none of them," said Nicholas shaking his head. "After a few days from when we saw their bloody meal, we saw another bloody mess made of snow, blood, human body parts and clothing by which we were able to recognize the criminals. Around this mess were a lot of prints of a wild animals and one of the members of our group identified that the prints belonged to bears and said that during this season, they were especially wild and angry, and could easily attack people. They have such sharp claws that they can easily rip a person in half."

"What happened to you next?" Coeus asked with intense curiosity. It seemed that everybody was so intent on finding out what happened next. Even the prosecutor, who was poised to object to anything possible, was now sitting with big, round eyes waiting to know more of Grandfather Nicholas' adventure.

"Next, everything seemed as if in a wonderful and pleasant dream. I started feeling better and healthier. Even though Norwegians are emotionless people, yet they're very kind and treated us with boiled fish. My friend and I even gained weight. After some time we received legal documents, new passports and new names, but staying in Norway was still dangerous and that's why we decided to move to the US. We waited for Spring so that the roads would clear. We rode to the first port which had a ship sailing to the US. I remember how tough it was for me to leave this country because I knew that I would never be able to return. I remember on the shore there were a few Norwegians who waved at us, as if they had known us for a long while. They looked like my relatives who lived back in Russia. The first thing I did when I reached the U.S. was that I tried to remember the machine for the healing treatment using precious stones, but in the U.S. no one really got interested in my invention. My son who tried to help me with the laboratory died by accident with his wife, and the only hope I had was my grandson, Adam, who was a school boy at that time. My health wasn't good and I knew I had to hurry. I tried to give Adam every detail and sketches of this machine and Adam promised me that he would continue my work. After many years, I passed away. I was happy when I found out that Adam received two degrees in order to continue my invention. I hoped that in the U.S. in the land of opportunities, Adam wouldn't suffer those obstacles which I faced back in the Soviet Union. But still, Adam had to face some issues. I guess it's the destiny of all inventors who are trying to invent something that would help people of the world," Grandfather Nicholas concluded sadly.

The court was quiet and the judge turned to Arianna, who was already offering her expertise.

"Arianna, are you ready to show Nicholas' aura again?"

Yes," Arianna answered and waved her hand, making an arc above Nicholas' head and at that very moment, the audience was awed to see how pure, clean and shimmering Nicholas' aura was. Everybody knew that an aura of light golden color meant the purity and truth of what Nicholas was telling.

Adam began little by little to understand what was happening here. Only now he realized that none of the court participants went through the oath and swearing in to tell the truth and nothing but the truth as it was usually done in earthly courts.

"Thank you," gladly said Kumbi to Arianna. "We can see that we can believe what Nicholas told us same as before. Now we are ready to hear our defendants."

"Your honor, we cannot hear them now," prosecutor stated with care; "since according to our court regulations that because they don't live in heaven and were not the petitioners for this level court, they can be questioned only without their awareness, meaning during their sleep and/or when they are in a coma. Since they are both healthy, we will have to wait a couple of more hours for them to fall asleep completely."

"Oh yes," agreed Kumbi, and his two advisors also nodded as well. "Let's have a break for an hour and then we will continue the trial."

Adam turned around and saw that the audience disappeared and only the cartoonist, Granny-Boxes and Adam's grandfather were still sitting there. Adam hurried to talk to his grandfather.

"Grandfather, it is a miracle that I can see you," Adam exclaimed running up to him.

"I am also very glad to see you my dear grandson," Nicholas said with excitement. "We have many things to discuss."

Adam knew that after the trial, his grandfather would disappear just like the audience and hence, he didn't know how to start a conversation. And instead of a normal talk, he had a bunch of phrases that he spoke together without really thinking them through.

"Grandmother died after a year since you died… The tree next to our house which was leaning finally fell on our house and destroyed our roof. Do you remember the dog which ran away on the day of my birthday? She returned after many years very dirty and skinny. The laboratory which I worked in burned down. Do you remember the beryl I took from your chest? I hid it under a big rock next to the fence, I had a sort of a buried treasure there.… During the graduation ceremony, when I was getting my Master's Degree in Geology, I thought I saw you. Was it really you? Tell me, did you see Stalin in heaven? I am so happy that you came here to help me. I wouldn't have been able to defeat Ali Baster and his accomplice Lampoon all alone." He held his grandfather by the hand and asked, "Do you think after the trial, we will be able to see each other again, on earth?"

Grandfather just smiled at Adam and didn't speak. Finally he answered, "My dear Adam, I was and always will be next to you. It's just that sometimes, you will notice me near by. But probably after this trial, something will change."

The break time flew fast and Grandfather thought it was very funny when Adam suggested going to a buffet and having a drink.

"Well, why not?" Adam asked with surprise. "Or don't they have a buffet here? I thought every court did."

"Yes, there is a buffet. I was there when I was here the first time, but believe me it is very boring there. Lawyers from every floor of the court are bragging among themselves how many cases they have won as if they're having a competition. The TV which is hanging on the wall makes predictions of the color of the dress in which Themis is going to appear at the next trial. But most of all, they like to make jokes about our judge Kumbi who cannot judge if he doesn't undo every button which is sewed on his cloak."

"Buttons?" Adam asked surprised.

"Yes, buttons. Didn't you notice that during the trial, his hands are always on his belly. When he is thinking about something, he undoes his buttons. People say that after the trial, when he rises from his seat, all the buttons fall on the floor. That's why his name is Kumbi."

Adam smiled and laughed about such aspect of Kumbi. He felt a certain ease because such a powerful and tremendously giant justice of heaven's chancellery is after all as little as a button on Kumbi's cloak.

Then Adam noticed that Grandfather was looking away and saw that someone was coming towards them. He moved to see who it was and saw a woman in her mid-40's who had light brown hair twisted into a bun. Adam was astonished by her sad yet beautiful green eyes. He noted to himself that her eyes were of a beautiful emerald green. The woman came closer to them and as if reading what he thought, raised her hand and said, "Yes my dear Adam, emerald is my lucky stone."

Adam was a bit lost and looked at Grandfather. Then Grandfather said, "Adam, I would like you to meet Maria Markovsky."

"Oh, it's you, that young woman..." Adam exclaimed excitedly. "Oh, you are here too..." Adam continued, "You came here because of me too..."

Yes, Adam," I will be the next witness for questioning but before that I have a very important mission because only you will be able to go back to earth. Unfortunately, I have no one else to ask to complete this mission."

"Oh, of course, anything," Adam answered confidently.

"The thing is that I have a grand-granddaughter and unfortunately she is now in one of the orphanages in New York and I would really appreciate it if you would adopt her and raise her."

"Yes, of course," Adam answered, "but again, in an orphanage?"

"Oh yes, as you know my daughter was in an orphanage, but after she immigrated to U.S. she got into an accident and now my grand-granddaughter has the same fate."

"But what is her name?"

"Unfortunately, the names of the Markovsky family were erased, and in order to survive my daughter and grand-granddaughter had to change their names. Now I don't know under what name she goes."

"But how will I able to find her?" Adam wondered.

"You will able to find her by her emerald green eyes which are passed on by females through the generations. We received this gift from nature and it is so strong that in our family no girl has been born with a different eye color. I'll tell you more, it was recommended for women of our generation to wear green clothes. That's why we were the beauties at every ball, because we'd have very elegant green dresses with jewelry made of green emeralds of various tones which exactly matched the color of our eyes. Believe me, we had lots of men going crazy for our beauty," laughed Maria.

"I will definitely find your grand-granddaughter," promised Adam, "and thank you for coming to the hearing," said Adam and elegantly kissed her hand.

Grandfather took her by the hand and led her to her seat. Only then Adam noticed how graciously she walked and that she was in a beautiful green outfit.

Then as before, out of nowhere, a voice loudly announced, "The court will continue the hearing! Everybody, take your seats!

The court room was filled in an instant. Judge Kumbi looked at Coeus and said,

"I believe you have another witness for questioning, if the prosecutor doesn't have objections."

Ipsos was astonished by Nicholas' life and he just quietly said, "No objection, your honor."

Then Kumbi told the secretaries to invite the witness Maria Markovsky

Maria stood on the marble platform and Coeus began his questioning, "Are you confirming Nicholas' words?"

"Yes I confirm them," Maria quietly answered.

"What can you tell us in confirmation of the facts brought here by Nicholas?"

"Only about my life," simply answered Maria, who then shifted her weight to stand more comfortably and began telling her story.

"I was born into the family of Count Markovsky in Northern Kavkaz, Russia. Our ancestors were very wealthy and came from Poland at the beginning of the 19th century. They had a number of tanneries factories and their business was always prospering. However, the main castle was located in Poland. My parents told me that the castle had an enormous Corinthian pediment and had a beautiful and an endless marble staircase. After the Revolution of 1917, all of our factories, property and money were forcibly taken away by the Communists. But that wasn't the end; they began shooting members of our family because they didn't want to belong to a Communist Party. My mother wasn't left anything to do but to move to another city and hide in a little village and buy fake documents which stated that she was a daughter of a poor peasant. This was a lie for survival. She shouldn't be judged for that because otherwise we wouldn't have survived. It was wartime and the only way to survive and save your family was to get a new name. Only because of these documents was I able to get a medical education and become a doctor in the hospital. When I turned 18, my mother right before her death gave me a little treasure box with the family treasures that were fortunately saved by her. I was very surprised why my mother didn't decide to sell at least one of the stones, so that the family would have money for food. Even if we were in need, my mother still treasured this box and when she gave the box to me she said that these stones would bring me luck. She told me not to ever sell them, but pass them from one generation to the next."

"How did you decide to show this box to Nicholas?" asked Coeus.

"As you know, Nicholas accidentally saw this box and I didn't have any other choice. Plus, I was very happy when I found out that my stones would help heal soldiers. I believe that the invention which Nicholas created would have been helpful for treating people if the KGB hadn't confiscated the invention and the stones. I didn't think that this would turn out to be very dangerous for us and was sure that I would able to have the stones back. I wanted to pass them on to my daughter, but due to fate I couldn't keep my promise which I made to my mother."

"When you started to reside in heaven's chancellery, were you able to find out the fate of the treasure box?" asked Coeus.

"No," answered Maria. "The KGB archives are so secretive that even from here I can't see their secret places. I guess they are stowed away too far in the underground and you need special access there, but I don't want to die a second time to get this access," finished Maria.

"Are there any other questions for Maria?" asked Kumbi.

"I have a question," said Ipsos. "You knew that your mother lied and made forged document, and you covered for her? Therefore, you are her accomplice in crime."

"I object," said Coeus. "This is not related to the matter of this case. Plus, by the law of heaven's chancellery, the child is not responsible for her parents' lie."

"Sustained," said Kumbi.

"However, you know that according to the heaven chancellery's justice guidelines, if someone has lied, then the karma for seven generations will be worsened."

"Objection! Objection," Coeus exclaimed and stood up from his seat. "We cannot use this guideline rule in this case because here Maria is a witness, not a defendant or a plaintiff."

The prosecutor jumped from his seat and exclaimed, "But how can we know if she is speaking the truth right now?"

Kumbi unscrewed another button on his mantle and by his face it was obvious that he didn't like this debate and he screamed, "Order! Order in my courtroom! We have Arianna to show us that. Only then can we apply any guidelines if necessary."

Coeus couldn't stop and still continued screaming, "And please don't forget, Ipsos, the presumption of innocence is still in effect."

"If nobody else has any questions, let's call Arianna," said Kumbi.

Arianna glided through the courtroom and took her spot at the other marble stands. She again made an arc above Maria's head and showed to everybody in the courtroom that her aura was light golden color, which meant that what she was speaking the truth. However, Ipsos was still trying to make his point and said, "Arianna was doing an expertise of an aura, which is not enough in this case. I motion to make an expertise of her karma."

To which the audience was in an uproar like a beehive. Judge Kumbi's eyes were big and round, like big and black buttons. Both of his advisors, who had been very calm all this time, also changed. One of them started laughing while the other started crying. Sisters Vivimas with shaking hands began flipping the jelly papers of guidelines to see if there were any cases with a similar precedent. Only Coeus seemed to be calm in this uproar.

Stressing each word he said, "Today among contemporary sources of law, there are no ways which would give an expertise of karma."

"Sustained," said Kumbi, then looked at Ipsos and said, "I suggest that if you are trying to make a point, make a reasonable one, Ipsos."

Ipsos got as red as a tomato and just flopped in his seat. He felt very embarrassed and sat quietly without looking at the judge. At this moment, a thought like a shadow passed over everybody in the courtroom—the prosecution would lose this case.

But neither Themis nor Kumbi paid attention to the shadow of thought. Kumbi continued the hearing and said, "I believe it's time to call and question both defendants."

Ipsos' eyes flickered and he answered, "I just checked that the defendants are in a deep sleep; hence, we can start the questioning."

"Well, then proceed. Let's begin with Mr. Ali Baster," Kumbi said and looked at Themis.

Themis stood up honorably and it seemed to Adam that she looked like Lady Liberty. She raised her hand and made a circle in the air and on the little marble platform right next to Arianna, Mr. Ali Baster appeared. Adam was hurt seeing him again, but he tried not to show his emotions on his face. For the first time, Adam saw Mr. Ali Baster in such a condition. He had disheveled hair; he wore baby blue pajamas and was sucking his left thumb. This habit had stayed with him ever since he was a baby and every time when he would go to sleep, he would suck his thumb. The judge's left-side advisor, Synaisthema, started laughing very cheerfully. Her laughter was very childlike, so everybody smiled as well, except for Kumbi's right-side advisor, Mello. This whole time, she had the same emotionless face, as she was always thinking.

"Mr. Ali Baster," Kumbi said looking at the defendant, "you are currently at the seventh level heaven chancellery as a defendant in the case of Mr. Adam, your ex-subordinate. Are you aware of this?"

Mr. Ali Baster took his left thumb from his mouth and began looking around the court without understanding where he was but said, "Hey, that's cool; I'm in heaven's chancellery. Whatever it is, I'm not guilty, and, Judge, I think we can talk this over, you know, privately."

The whole audience starting laughing very loudly and Themis started laughing as well. Though the whole trial she had been quiet, she now exclaimed, "I should've gone to earth's court more often. People can be so funny out there; they think that Judges rule in the court… if they bribe the judge they may get the justice they want." As she was laughing, her earrings dangled and the light beamed from her earrings that made her look even more mesmerizing.

Kumbi waited a few seconds, for the audience to finish their laughing and then continued, "Mr. Ali Baster, the plaintiff, Adam, is accusing you of causing him moral damage by disturbing him while he was working on his invention; you defamed his honor, dignity and business reputation and plagiarized his ideas. Are you affirming these facts?"

"No, I do not," Ali Baster angrily exclaimed. He came closer to the Judge and whispered to him, "Let's talk, privately."

Kumbi didn't like Mr. Ali Baster's behavior and he began saying, "Mr. Ali Baster, follow the order in the court. Go back to your stand next to Arianna."

At the same moment, Coeus asked, "What do you have to prove that the amazing machine for treating people was created by you?"

"I invented this machine," angrily screamed Ali Baster, "because I am smarter than Adam and the whole world will praise me!" he continued screaming.

"Objection, your honor, we cannot take Mr. Ali Baster's words in seriousness because he may be still suffering from the shock that he is in heaven's chancellery," prosecutor Ipsos quickly pointed out.

"Well, let the expertise be conducted. Arianna, do your job, and show us whether Ali Baster is in shock, and let us also see what aura he has," the judge said.

Arianna gladly stood at the center of the big marble stand, and asked Ali Baster to stand in the center of the smaller marble stand. Then she raised her hand on Ali Baster's head and in an instant a dark purple aura began to beam above the defendant's head. A wave of awe came across the audience and some people even stood up from the back row to see the color better, and everybody understood that the dark purple aura meant that the defendant was lying. Coeus stood up from his seat and said, "Your honor, please take into account the fact that Mr. Ali Baster's aura was not just purple but dark purple. Such a level of lie is rarely seen in our court."

To which the judge answered, "Well, I take your remark into account, however, (he quietly said) don't forget that Mr. Ali Baster is working in an administrative job where lying is necessary and has to be part of one's personality."

"Your honor, I would like to note that after a couple of minutes Mr. Ali Baster will get a call from which he will wake up, hence I think it's time to let him go," prosecutor Ipsos said.

"No objections," Kumbi said.

And at the same instant, Mr. Ali Baster disappeared from the little marble stand as if he had never been there.

"The next defendant is Mr. Lampoon, who needs to be questioned," said the Judge.

And after a few seconds the courtroom saw the journalist Lampoon. He wore only underwear imprinted with pictures of dollars. He had little eyes that would swiftly look left or right. Judge Kumbi looked at him and said,

"Mr. Lampoon, you are in the seventh level of heaven's chancellery and are accused of causing moral damage to Mr. Adam by writing and publishing a series of articles slandering Mr. Adam, by the order of Mr. Ali Baster, who has paid you an amount of $3000. Do you agree with this account of the facts?"

"Oh, my god, what luck, I am one of the luckiest journalists ever! I've climbed up to heaven's chancellery," the journalist exclaimed happily.

He ran up to the prosecutor Ipsos who was close to him, and tried to take off his mantle. This astonished the court. No one could understand what he was doing. The judge began to scream, "Order in the court. Mr. Lampoon, why are you taking off Ipsos' mantle and cap."

"Are you that stupid? You think I can report my findings in my underwear?" rhetorically asked Lampoon.

"Be quiet, Lampoon," the judge screamed. Meanwhile, Lampoon pushed Ipsos down on the floor, and took away his cap. The bailiff went to help the prosecutor by fighting with Lampoon to take away the cap. However, judge Kumbi screamed, "Let him have the cap, we need to continue the questioning."

Lampoon happily ran back to the small stand next to Arianna and the audience finally saw him standing in underwear imprinted with dollars and Ipsos' cap with the golden tassel that Lampoon had to constantly blow away from his left eye.

Coeus continued the questioning, "Do you agree that every word which you wrote in your articles was a lie about Adam from which you received a profit?"

Mr. Lampoon very calmly answered, "It depends what you mean by truths and lies. We journalists have always been dependent on people who pay us money. We've always written and will always write what people want to hear from us. If we only wrote the truth, the whole world would go crazy. That's why I was only doing my job," answered Mr. Lampoon, "especially, because such a big amount is rarely offered."

Kumbi looked at the prosecutor and wanted to ask whether he had any objections, but when he saw that Ipsos wore an angry face after Lampoon took away his cap, he decided not to. He then, asked Arianna to offer expertise of Lampoon's aura. Arianna as always elegantly moved her hand over Lampoon's head and everyone in the court saw that Lampoon's aura was dark green.

"Oh, god," someone from the audience said, "his aura will always be as heavy as the weight of the money."

After a few minutes, since he wasn't necessary, Mr. Lampoon disappeared just like the previous defendant.

"Will there be any remarks, objections or comments from any of the court participants?" Kumbi asked loudly. Only the sound of pencil on paper was heard. The cartoonist was finishing his portraits. "Well, then the court will go into conference."

The courtroom was still quiet, as it seemed that no one was in a hurry and everybody was waiting for the decision. Coeus believed that he would win, while Arianna, as always, was proud that she was able to show the magnificence of her colors to the audience. The Sisters Vivimas like the other secretaries took off their shoes, which had been hurting their feet, and then they were trying to find where their right and left shoes were under the desk. The bailiff really wanted to go to a buffet, and drink something, as he would usually do after each trial. The Granny-Boxes impatiently waited for the decision, because they wanted to later gossip about it with heaven's inhabitants. The cartoonist didn't really worry about anything, and only looked at his hands holding a pencil and how they moved on the paper. Adam and Grandfather Nicholas wanted to have a little more time after the trial in order to talk. Prosecutor Ipsos had the saddest face in the courtroom. He felt as if he had lost his head with his favorite cap. Meanwhile, Granny-Boxes started chattering with other Grannies who came to see the trial. They started chattering about each of the court participants and Adam overheard their conversation.

"They have been out for a while now, usually they don't take so long to make a decision," said one of the Grannies.

"Oh, every decision on the 7th level in heaven's chancellery depends on buttons and tears," said another Granny and all of them started laughing.

"Oh, tell me more," said the new Granny, who only recently started visiting trials. She was quite different from other Grannies because her hair had only a few shades of grey.

"Oh, let me begin the story," said the bigger Granny-Box. "Before coming here, Judge Kumbi used to work as an apprentice in a tailor shop. People say he was a good helper and dreamed of sewing beautiful camisoles. However, he wasn't even allowed to take scissors to cut the material. The only thing he could do is to sew buttons to the finished clothing. Years passed by and Kumbi sewed thousands of buttons, but he was no nearer to his dream. Once, in their tailor shop a Judge came in to order to have a shirt for outings. Kumbi tried really hard for the Judge to like him and very accurately sewed the buttons on his camisole. In order to look meaningful, Kumbi gave a compliment to the judge and said, *'You are probably a very busy and wise man to make decisions about people's lives.'* The Judge admired himself in the mirror and said *'Oh yes, little friend, judging is not the same as sewing buttons.'* After which Kumbi got upset and secretly started dreaming about becoming a judge."

"As you see, his dream came true," said the smaller Granny-Box. "But I guess he couldn't stop his old habit," she said with a smirk.

"Oh yes," said one of the Grannies, "our habits are very constant, they follow us whichever level of heaven we get to. For many years, I have seen many things. People changed their status, social class, appearance, and even professions once they come here, but their habits are still with them."

"Oh yes, I absolutely agree with you." continued another chatter-box. "For example, Kumbi's left-side advisor Synaisthema, when she was assigned to work here on the seventh level, though warned by Themis a couple of times, she couldn't leave behind her habits from earth. People say a few hours before she came here, she was about to get married and was a beautiful bride. She really loved her groom. However, on the day of the wedding, she found out about him cheating with her sister Mello, who is also Kumbi's advisor on the right."

"No," said another Granny-box, "Mello is not her sister; you're mixing up everything because you're so old. Her sister wouldn't be in here because she cheated with her groom. She is under another department."

"In another court," said another Granny-box.

"Of course not," answered another chatter-box, "she will be working in the laundry room for eternity because she is trying to wash away her sin."

"Oh, now I get why Synaisthema both cries and laughs like all brides at their weddings from all the stress. That's how Synaisthema is for her eternal life, laughing due to happiness that she was getting married to the man she loved, and crying because he cheated on her."

"But if there were no marriages, there wouldn't be any cheating," said another chatter-box.

"Then what is Mello's story?" curiously asked a smaller Granny-Box.

"She was also a bride before she got here," said one Granny.

"Oh, Kumbi is sitting between two brides." laughed one chatter-box. "I imagine what the justice of this is."

"Well, Kumbi when making a decision relying only on his buttons while advisors are needed for emotions. Where else will he find a splash of emotions but from the brides?"

"But what happened to Mello?" curiously asked the smaller Granny-box again.

"First of all Mello was never getting married," began to say the oldest Granny-box.

"How come? I remember I saw her the day she came up here, she was wearing a wedding dress with a veil," exclaimed one chatter-box.

"Oh, let me tell you her story. You don't know what happened so be quiet and just listen," the oldest Granny-box smirked. "Anyway, the angel who accompanied Mello from earth told me that Mello had everything in her life. She had a career, money, prestigious job, but she never had true love. She thought that it is just a waste of time and based everything on reason rather than feelings. By the end of her life she felt sorry that she never loved and wasn't loved by anyone. That's why before her death, she asked people to bury her in a wedding dress."

"Oh, why a sad story," said a little granny-box whipping a tear away. "Then she never had a true love's kiss."

"As well everything that goes after that," laughed one granny whose cheeks were as pink as cupcakes.

"Oh, look, even after coming here, she still continues to base everything on reason," concluded the smallest Granny-box.

After a short time, Kumbi with his two advisors returned to the courtroom. Kumbi began his statement in a loud voice, "The Court under me, Kumbi, my two advisors, Mello and Synaisthema, reviewed a case regarding the compensation for moral damage of Mr. Adam, and have decided to approve the plaintiff's petition and compensate his moral damage. We're giving him one of the high-ranking compensations and the sixth sense and also an ability to have once in a life-time wings so that he will able to return home by himself. Plus, noting the mitigating factors, Adam was under the influence of messenger Ptiscy and therefore committed disorderly conduct, hence, the earthly charge is considered nullified. From people's memory as well as from Albany's computer base, this incident will be erased. Finally, we just received a decision from the 3rd level "miscarriage of justice court" who approved Adam's request regarding the exoneree Peter. This time they decided to make an exception and give him the chance to meet his son."

The audience began to applaud. Many people began coming up to Adam, hugging him, shaking his hand, congratulating him for winning the case. After which, one after the other they disappeared. Coeus, standing next to Adam also received congratulations from the audience and promised to Adam that in some time, they would meet again. Adam was really afraid that Grandfather Nicholas would also disappear just like the others, so he hurried to begin a conversation with his grandfather.

"Grandpa, will you help me with the invention? Now I believe that I can continue my research, right?" Adam asked hopefully.

"I will always be near you," Grandpa answered, "and I am blessing you with continuing to work on the invention."

"Well, maybe you'll be allowed, at least sometimes, to come on earth."

"No, honey, I didn't reach that level yet. I don't have such permission, to move between earth and heaven, like others here who are allowed to. My time is expiring." He hugged Adam and disappeared with Maria who was standing next to him.

Adam sat on one of the benches and took his head in his hands, not knowing what to do next. Then he heard a sound of footsteps coming towards him. He turned around and saw Themis. She was smiling as she had before, and it was obvious that she was happy for Adam.

"And I won't see you again," Adam said sadly.

"Who knows…?" Themis said, "Maybe someday…I sometimes, go down there."

"Well, how do I go down there, and return home?" asked Adam.

Themis laughed and answered, "You have wings on your back—just fly!"

At the same moment, Adam felt pain on both sides of his shoulder blades. It was as if something was growing from within his spine. After a few minutes, he saw magnificent, giant, white wings.

"Do you like your wings? Do you feel comfortable in them?" asked Themis.

"Oh, my god, I have the same wings as Ptiscy."

He tried to fly, reached Kumbi's chair, fell, then saw that under Kumbi's chair there were buttons on the floor; then he flew to the right, hit some flower pots, which broke, and finally went up.

"Goodbye, Themis," Adam exclaimed from above.

He saw how Themis was quietly waving to him. He realized that he was flying higher and higher, since Themis was getting smaller and smaller…

NOTES

1. LAMPOON—from the Greek, means slander.
2. KUMBI—from the Greek, means button.
3. MELLO—from the Greek, means mind.
4. SYNAISTHEMA—from the Greek, means sentimental.
5. ANTHROPOS—from the Greek, means man/human.
6. KAKO—from the Greek, means evil.

Chapter Eleven

The N.Y. Supreme Court

Losing a Winning Case

Adam woke up in the morning because a light beam was shining on his eyes through an open window. It seemed weird to him, since he usually closed his windows before going to sleep. He stretched and screamed from pain in his spine, and he thought that he must have broken his spine. He dragged himself to the bathroom and when he looked in the mirror he gasped. Both of his shoulder blades had bright red bruises. Adam began to remember what had happened. Everything seemed like a dream to him: Themis, Grandfather Nicholas, heaven's chancellery…he felt dizzy. He hurried to his living room and saw that on the table there were two pictures which were drawn with a pencil. One of them was his portrait and on the second was his grandfather. He took these portraits, sat on a sofa and started looking at them. At the bottom left corner, there was a tiny signature, "Cartoonist of Heaven's Chancellery." His heart trembled when he realized that he would never again see Grandfather Nicholas and Themis the woman of unearthly beauty. However, he became happy because his offenders Ali Baster and Lampoon were punished for their wrongdoings by heaven's chancellery and would get what they deserved. Adam approached the window, and was looking at the sky with a desire to go back up there. Everything on earth seemed to him uninteresting and primitive. Adam laughed to himself and continued his train of thought, remembering what happened yesterday.

"Everybody says that the American System of Justice is the most perfect in the world. Well, maybe, maybe…However, it also has loop holes… it would have been better if they would learn from heaven's chancellery which doesn't have any mistakes. But if I told anyone about my adventure, people on earth would just think I'm crazy."

After a couple of days, Adam received a letter from the Supreme Court that said that his case would not be reviewed by the Supreme Court because the court decided that the appellate court didn't make any mistakes and because his case didn't seem to be vitally important. It was recommended that he come to the Supreme Court to pick up his documents. In order to make him feel happy, Adam ordered a car service called "Phaeton" to take him to the Supreme Court, but the driver didn't look like Amaxas.

In the Supreme Court, there was an endless amount of lines for different windows, dialogs with clerks who wore plain and bored faces. Adam wanted to again have the same feelings which he had when he met Ptiscy on the roof. He went by the similar hallway in order to find the same staircase; he saw that there were no staircases at all. At first, he thought he must have gone down the wrong corridor, so he went by other ones, but then realized that he wasn't wrong. The security guard, an elderly man, noticed that Adam was lost and asked, "What are you looking for?"

Adam showed him to a space in the hallway and said that there must be a staircase which leads to the roof of the Supreme Court. To which the security laughed and said, "Man, I have worked here over 15 years and believe me, there was never a staircase here to the roof. There is only one staircase that leads to the roof, but you can only get there from the basement, and that door is always closed."

Adam didn't want the guard to finish his sentence, because he saw the elevator doors open and a familiar face. Coeus was coming towards him, his counsel from heaven's chancellery.

"Coeus, my friend, you're here, I'm so happy," Adam exclaimed.

To which Coeus just placed a finger to his lips. Adam followed Coeus along.

"You're here because of me?" Adam asked.

"No, my dear friend, this time, I'm not here for you," Coeus kindly answered. "I'm here for another case regarding the compensation for moral damage to one needy immigrant whose book was published by another person."

"But I am sure that if you are her counsel, then her petition will be satisfied in the Supreme Court. But you see, my case wasn't even reviewed by the Supreme Court," Adam said sadly showing the papers to Coeus.

"My dear Adam, each case is unique and it is mistaken to think that all cases can be judged the same. The needy immigrant could not be invited to the seventh level of heaven's chancellery because of her wealth of imagination. That's why Kumbi sent me to her, here to earth. By the way, here on earth, I have a different name, here I am Leonard. Plus, don't you remember one of the most important rules in heaven's chancellery, "if the moral damage was compensated in heaven's chancellery, then on earth no compensation will be approved and vice versa."

Adam stood and absorbed all the information that Coeus told him and it was obvious that he wanted to ask about something, but was shy. Finally, he asked, "How is she?"

"Oh, Themis?" kindly said Coeus. "She as always is spreading her charms and justice. I will definitely say hi to her from you."

Adam just quietly shook his head and didn't want to say anything else.

"Well, it time for me to go," Coeus said. "I have things to do." He disappeared in the same elevator from which he had come.

Chapter Twelve

Hoop-la around the Cap with a Tassel

Coeus wasn't the only one who came down to earth from heaven's chancellery during these days. There was a debate of sending prosecutor Ipsos on earth as well. The problem consisted of the following. It is not often in the court practice of heaven's chancellery the court participants who were invited from earth were allowed to take any objects from heaven's chancellery with them. If that were to happen in rare cases, then these objects were to be immediately taken back to heaven's chancellery. When such an object was taken to earth from heaven, an energy funnel would open. This funnel would cause a leak of energy. This was a very dangerous situation for both the heaven chancellery and the inhabitants of earth because the information that both parties shouldn't know about might leak out. Especially, in regards to the seventh level of heaven's chancellery, not by chance was it placed on the highest floor. Such situations did occur in heaven's chancellery at various level and they were usually referred to as "miscarriages of justice."

Usually, only a few court participants would know about these leaks, mostly judges and Themis herself. This information was not spread around the heaven's chancellery, so that no one would panic. This was reasonable because every day in courts, every participant has to be calm in order to conduct the procedure accurately.

After when Adam's case was solved and everybody was talking about his triumphant winning. Everybody got tired so much and almost forgot that the journalist Lampoon disappeared from the court, with Ipsos' cap. Plus, can you believe it; Ipsos had already been to a couple of hearings while only wearing a mantle. Only when at one of the hearings, when Ipsos confessed that he could not make fair decisions without his cap because then he felt brainless, only then did everybody notice that he was missing a cap.

Of course, Coeus was the happy one in this issue because then he had an ability to ask for a review of previous cases because in court regulations, it was vividly stated that "prosecuting brainlessly is prohibited." But Kumbi was the one who took his head in his hands. He was very worried that such leak occurred on their level and Themis of course would note Kumbi's ignorance, and in the next century, he might not be reappointed for the position. He was thoughtfully sitting in his office and looked very worried. He would sew the buttons on his mantle, then he would take them off. Both of his assistants quietly peeked through his door and decided not to talk to him. They knew he was about to have a serious talk with Themis. However, the conversation with Themis was very short.

Themis, who enthusiastically tended to protect the heaven's chancellery from all the leaks made a decision to send Ipsos himself for his cap because it was his fault and he improperly didn't get it back. After a few seconds, Ipsos was immediately sent to earth. He landed on one of the streets in New York and because of his clothes looked very unusual. It was hard to understand, whether he was a professor from a graduation ceremony because of his robe, or was he returning from exercising because he was wearing tennis shoes and activewear under his mantle. Plus, across his spine a carpet for yoga or pilates was hanging. Basically, it was obvious that this man had a very busy lifestyle; he was prepared for attending a graduation ceremony, exercising and relaxing in yoga.

After landing, Ipsos started nagging passers by asking them if they knew a journalist by the name of Lampoon who took his cap with a golden tassel during the trial. However, New Yorkers would very quickly say that they hadn't and swiftly disappeared. That's because the population of New York is a special category of people. It consists of New Yorkers, tourists and immigrants who come from different countries. In this group, there are mostly tourists and immigrants. That's why it's understandable that tourists didn't know English, in which language Ipsos was asking them about his cap, but at least they took a few photos with him. Immigrants knew English, but very badly, and that's why they barely understood Ipsos and finally only a few immigrants understood the word "cap" and would offer their own to him, but he would say no. New Yorkers would perfectly understand Ipsos; however, then would talk so fast that only other New Yorkers could understand them and not people from other places. New Yorkers not only talk fast but also walk fast. They are one of the busiest groups of people in the world. They work at two or even three jobs. Sometimes, it seems that they can extend the day for more than 24 hours in order to make more money. New Yorkers can work in different boroughs and for extra hours of work, then can drive for more hours than what the job entails. That's why they are not looking around, they look only straightforwardly and honestly, and don't care who is passing them on the street and they have a special ability to look through the passersby. New Yorkers won't be surprised by weird clothing or behavior, because they have seen a lot. That's why they are very tolerant and calm.

Basically, Ipsos didn't get any information from the people passing on the streets and so he just wandered around. By the end of the day he had a couple of hats which he got from enthusiastic passersby and different business cards and flyers where they gave information about where to get free immigration services, a sale in Macys, and a contest to win free pizza at Columbus Circle.

By the end of the day, Ipsos ended up in a hospital in a psychiatric department. We don't know exactly how, but probably one of the passersby brought him there or he was just given an address and he went there himself.

The nurse listened to Ipsos' story, and surprisingly just wrote down a few things, filled out an application, took his weight and height. However, when she started measuring his pulse and blood pressure, she noticed that he didn't have them. The nurse thought that maybe the sphygmomanometer is broken and went to get another one. Meanwhile Ipsos, who didn't like these procedures, went out and started walking around the hospital. Later, Ipsos felt tired and very sleepy. In one of the rooms he saw an empty bed, undressed, dressed up in the hospital gown that was lying on the bed and went to sleep.

Ipsos woke up from a very bright light. He squinted his eyes and realized that he was naked and lying on some kind of a table. It was very cold and a few people were bent over him wearing white gowns and caps. Ipsos thought that he had reached the first level of heaven's chancellery – again; where they sort out people and send them to specific levels. But then he noticed that these people's faces were half-covered with white masks, and as he remembered that was not the usual uniform in the first level of heaven's chancellery. One of them said to the other, "acute attack of appendicitis, we have to conduct an emergency operation." Ipsos wanted to ask them when and for what reason they made an addition to their uniform, but a needle painfully went into Ipsos' vein and before he could react, he fell asleep.

He woke up lying in bed in another room; he was very nauseated and had a major headache. His lower right side of the stomach was hurting. He couldn't move. Then the nurse came and asked him, "What is your name? Where do you live? I can't find your folder"

"My name is Ipsos. I live in heaven's chancellery."

"Alright, heaven's chancellery, what's the number?" asked the nurse.

"Seventh level," Ipsos said.

"What's the borough and zip-code?" the nurse pressed him.

"I don't know," honestly said Ipsos.

"Alright, but what is your insurance?" asked the nurse. "How are you planning to pay for your medical treatment?"

Ipsos was just blankly staring at the nurse. Finally she said, "If you don't have insurance, there is an insurance agency down the street and they can help you apply for Obamacare."

"I don't want to," Ipsos said and shook his head.

"You know that if you won't apply, you will have to pay a fine." she said with a strict voice.

Then she was called by another nurse and left.

Ipsos understood that something bad was going on with him or was about to happen. He didn't like the nurse; it seemed to him as if she was nagging at him, and she wasn't pretty and smelled badly. Ipsos didn't like such women. "She has a bad aura," thought Ipsos. "She's in the wrong place. This is not her favorite profession. She wanted to be a photographer, but because they don't get paid much, she started taking courses to become a nurse…To be a nurse is one of the most prestigious professions in New York, of course after a lawyer and a doctor." Pondering this, Ipsos, holding the right side of his belly, got up from bed and went for a walk in the hallway. Surprisingly, he later found the room where he went to sleep and in the closet were his clothes. He changed and came out through the backdoor where the garbage was usually taken out.

Ipsos again got out on the streets of New York. This time he was more fortunate. His goal was to complete his mission more accurately. He decided to ask assistance from his colleagues and began asking the passers-by how to get to the nearest court. People gladly pointed him directions to the court, and after a few hours he went into the building of the District Court.

In the entrance, Ipsos was stopped and asked a lot of unnecessary questions and he didn't like where this was all going already. He thought, "in our court it is much easier." People in uniforms asked him to unfold his carpet and he reluctantly agreed. But when they asked him to take off his tennis shoes, he got upset and screamed,

"I am a prosecutor, not a messenger angel who's walking barefoot. I don't have to take off my shoes."

Finally he was allowed to go inside. He walked through a long hallway and soon saw that in one of the rooms was a hearing. He went inside and was surprised that the construction of the courtroom looked different from heaven's chancellery. He thought that the way it was structured was not smart and didn't like it. However, he sat at the back of the courtroom and thought to wait for the prosecutor to ask him where to find journalist Lampoon. He started listening to the subject matter of the case and noticed that the defense attorney made a motion to reschedule the hearing because the defendant was having asthma attack. Ipsos looked at the poor defendant and saw that he was barely able to breathe. While the prosecutor began saying, "No, we don't have time for that. After this hearing, we have other three cases to hear." The prosecutor smirked and continued, "don't worry he'll be taken care of in prison, we have full medical coverage for people like him." Then Ipsos realized that the prosecutor was wrong. He raised his hand so that he would notice him. He wanted to explain to him that he was not allowed to do that and if Themis found out, she would be very upset. However, it seemed that the prosecutor didn't pay any attention to him. Then Ipsos stood up from his seat and started screaming: "This is a mistrial. I plead for the case to be reviewed again. In the name of Themis, you have to hear the case again."

At this moment, Ipsos saw that the judge was for some reason looking very angry and started hitting the table with a tiny wooden hammer and saying,

"Order, order in my court," and made a remark for Ipsos to get back in his seat.

Ipsos noticed that the judge didn't look like Kumbi at all and thought, "Oh, how is he judging? He doesn't even have buttons." It was obvious that the judge was trying to get calm and continue the hearing. However, Ipsos could not live with the injustice. He got up and started moving towards the prosecutor. At this moment, he saw that a bailiff and two court officers started running in his direction. They tried to grab Ipsos by his arms, but Ipsos was not letting go. He screamed, "I am prosecutor Ipsos from heaven's chancellery. You can't imagine how hard it must be for me. I have claustrophobia. You can't imagine how hard it is for me to get up on the seventh level every day. But I never made unjust decisions like you just did."

And that's how a fight broke out. The court officer pushed Ipsos to the floor and tried to twist his hands behind his back so he wouldn't fight back. After a few minutes, when they pulled Ipsos up from the floor, they noticed that there is a giant red stain on the right side of his mantle which got bigger and bigger. The courtroom was in a panic. There was a sound of "Oh, ah!" that went across the whole courtroom. People stoop up in the back rows to see what happened to Ipsos. Someone called 911, others screamed to call the ambulance. People were in a panic and one of the members of the audience who sat in the front row started telling to his neighbor, "Look, the court officers are out of their minds. They killed a man who was fighting for justice."

"No, they didn't kill him," the neighbor started objecting, "Fortunately, they only injured him."

To which one of them stood up to get a better look at the scene by raising his neck like a giraffe and said, "No, the officers couldn't have injured or killed him. They don't have any weapons to do that."

"Look better, maybe they have a knife or a gun."

"No, they don't have anything. But where did the blood come from? Maybe he injured himself?"

The two members of the audience were pondering.

Someone from the audience called the reporters from NY1 and after a few minutes, in the courtroom, there was a young lady, a reporter with a microphone, and a cameraman. The lady tried to conduct an interview with Ipsos, who was heavily bleeding. In this chaos no one noticed that the reporter came earlier than the police or the ambulance. After the reporter, the firefighters came. They calmly stood on the corner and were writing a report. After that they said that their machine showed no signs of fire and so they left.

At this moment, people who were in the courtroom were the witnesses of this tragic picture. When the reporter raised a mike to Ipsos, who was barely able to talk and had a puddle of blood around him, she asked him a couple of questions at the same time, "You too think that our judicial system is rotten?"

"Yes," shortly answered Ipsos. "I now understand why Themis keeps packing and unpacking her luggage.

The reporter didn't seem to notice his answer and continued, "Are you a representative of the program led by one of the candidates for the governor's election?"

"No, I am a representative from the heaven's chancellery. Kumbi sent me to get my cap."

The reporter enthusiastically continued and said, "Are you related to the actors who a couple of days ago, in angel costumes, were protesting against the current judicial system, and are representing a campaign program for justice?"

To which Ipsos blankly answered, "Justice can't be a temporary campaign program. Justice has to be eternal."

"Is your statement 'Justice has to be eternal' your new logo?"

But it seemed that Ipsos didn't know what she was talking about. After which the reporter continued, "You must be one of the enthusiastic activists of the program that you even decided to come to the courtroom and are dying here in the puddle of blood, so that the public and the government will think about making a reform of the judicial system."

But it seemed that Ipsos was not listening to her anymore. Thankfully, the police and ambulance rushed in and the reporter was pushed away from Ipsos.

"Oh," said Ipsos, "now I understand Lampoon's strong desire to give a report from heaven's chancellery. It even cost me my favorite cap."

"Lampoon, you said Lampoon," said the reporter. "So you know Lampoon?" The reporter got the feeling that she could get an extra point for that.

Later, Ipsos was put in the ambulance and was rushed away from the court building. Then poor Ipsos ended up in the same hospital from which he ran away earlier. The nurse who was at first registering Ipsos, didn't want to register him for the second time and worriedly said to her co-worker, "This is the person who doesn't have a blood pressure and a pulse. Remember I told you about him?"

Her co-worker, a nurse, who was a bit older, looked at her with pity and said, "You didn't have a vacation for a while. Let me talk to the supervisor so he'll give you a break. You really need one."

Somehow, Ipsos was taken to the surgery table and the nurse who smelled badly and wasn't pretty in Ipsos' opinion when seeing him shook her hands and screamed, "I told you to apply for the Obamacare health plan. But you just disappeared and now are again in trouble."

To which poor Ipsos hardly opened his eyes, looked at the nurse for a second time, and understood that he still didn't like her and said, "I don't want to be in trouble. I just want to find my cap."

"Then you have to apply for Obamacare," she started to say but she couldn't finish as a crowd of reporters rushed into the operation room. It was a news reporter from NY1 news who met Ipsos in the courtroom. The camera man as always was running after her and the last one was Lampoon.

"He's here, he's here, the prosecutor from heaven's chancellery," exclaimed Lampoon and pointed at Ipsos. "I told you the truth about visiting heaven's chancellery. None of you believed me."

After which he took the cameraman by his elbow screamed at him, "Take a close-up of him. Ipsos, Ipsos, say to the camera that I was telling the truth. I was there with you in the heaven's chancellery…a good place indeed."

Ipsos looked at him with such amazement that he couldn't hide his excitement that he finally found him. Lampoon kept yelling at Ipsos without noticing the nurse who asked them all to leave the building or she would call the security guards.

"Look, I even have your cap with me," said Lampoon

After which, Lampoon took the cap from the bag and put it on himself. Then he took the camera man by elbow and said, "Now take a close-up of me wearing his cap."

The young reporter finally was able to extend the mike to Ipsos and tried to ask him 100 questions a minute.

"So the candidate's campaign program is called 'Heaven's Chancellery'? Do you state that journalist Lampoon is part of your program? Who tried to assassinate you? Maybe the opponents of your candidate? Are you afraid that the present governor will arrest you and file a lawsuit against you?"

At the same time, the nurse screamed, "No, this is not good. Before he is going to get arrested, he has to pay the bill for the treatment he got here before. The heaven's chancellery is not important, what's important is that he doesn't have medical insurance to pay the bills."

Basically, everybody was screaming at the same time, even the cameraman who didn't like the fact that everybody was pulling him either right or left. At one moment, Ipsos seeing that Lampoon stood very close to him, grabbed the cap from his head, put it on himself, and disappeared in one glimpse. Kumbi kept his promise and after when Ipsos completed his mission, every human being who met Ipsos had their memories erased about him.

When Ipsos disappeared in front of a group of people, the journalists looked at the nurse, and asked, “What are we doing here? What can be interesting for the news in this hospital?”

The nurse answered, “Well, the garbage from the hospital is not taken out regularly and causes us problems.”

The journalists hurried to the garbage room, then took a video of big bags of garbage and surprised the rats that were having lunch. They found the custodian who was drunk and interviewed him. After which, happily they went to their work places.

Chapter Thirteen

Finding the Little Countess

A couple of months ago, Adam was trying to get used to the new feeling which he got after visiting the heaven's chancellery. A lot of things changed in his personality. What before looked important, now didn't have any value. Pain which followed him and was part of his life, now disappeared. The feeling of guilt that he couldn't continue his grandfather's invention also disappeared and wasn't eating his insides like a worm anymore. Sometimes in public he would see familiar faces which he saw at the trial. These people would smile and walk past him, but it seemed that none of them would remember that they were there.

One day on Broadway he saw a cartoonist who was drawing a portrait of a stranger. He came up to him hoping that he would recognize him, but the cartoonist just asked him if he wanted his portrait to be drawn. Adam said that he already has a portrait of him drawn by him, but the cartoonist just looked at Adam and said that he didn't remember that and just took the coins from the stranger whose portrait he finished drawing. Adam noticed that the cartoonist even had the same hands and a similar pencil which was sharpened on both ends; Adam had noticed this in the heaven's chancellery and thought it was weird.

In an information office, Adam saw secretaries at the front desk, two twin sisters. They were both wearing a similar dress in polka dots which the sisters Vivimas wore. Adam wanted to talk to them and came closer. When he saw their name tags he was surprised even more—their last name was Vivian; and he was astonished when he saw that one of the sisters took off her shoes because they were hurting, and hid her feet behind the chair. But the major factor which surprised him was when he obtained the information about all the orphanages in New York, he wanted to go out to the exit, but the door wasn't opening. Then one of the sisters came up to him and said, "Sorry, the door is jammed and opens only from the entrance. Can you please go to the other end of the hallway to exit?"

"How weird," said Adam, "so you have only one exit from the office?"

To which another sister laughed and said, "Of course only one, but if you'd have wings you'd go from a window."

This seemed funny to everybody in the office. Adam was looking at all of them and was laughing loudly as well, but he was laughing because a few months ago, he really did have wings and it really wasn't easy to fly with, as most people think.

Adam now had the list of all the orphanages and he really hoped that he would soon find the young Countess. Happily, while whistling to himself, he went outside and saw an address of an orphanage that wasn't far from this office. He went there, but when he came to the doors of the orphanage, he saw that it was the back door of a church. An elderly nun who came out at his knock on the door, looked at him with a question as to what was he asking. And truly, Adam's request was very strange, "I would like to find a girl from 10-15 years of age, who comes from a royal ancestry and has green eyes."

"Well, we have a lot of girls with green eyes. But first, why are you looking for her?" the nun asked and crossed her hands at her chest.

"Her grandmother asked me to find her," said Adam.

"Oh then, this won't take long. Let's go inside to the filing room and pull all the files of the girls."

Adam was surprised how the nun opened a heavy door bolt and that the door easily opened. He walked after the nun by the stairs going up and when they reached a room filled with shelves, then another nun who was a bit younger, a secretary, asked him if he had a written letter from the grandmother and the name of the grandmother, where she was born as well as where she currently resided. It was obvious that Adam was lost and the nuns noticed that and just looked at each other. After a few minutes, Adam stutteringly answered, "The name of the grandmother is Maria Markovsky, but she was forced to change her name many years ago. That's why I don't think we'll able to find the girl by this name. She was born in Russia, but her daughter immigrated here to the US; that's why the grand-granddaughter was probably born here."

"Where does the grandmother live now?" curiously asked the nuns to hopefully find something that might lead them to find the girl. To which Adam slowly answered,

"She, she…she, died, she died, in '45, in 1945. She was shot by the Communists."

"How was she able to give you a request," asked the nuns, who were now very suspicious of Adam and his intentions.

"We met recently, um, in the seventh level of heaven's chancellery, where I had a hearing of my case."

The room was all quiet. The nuns were pale and didn't know how to correctly react to what Adam told them. Finally, one of the nuns said, "My friend, I think we won't able to help you. I think you should leave the church. We have no right to judge you in anything. But we don't have the right to let you adopt a girl."

After a few minutes, Adam was outside of the church, on the noisy side of the street. He was so hurt because he knew that he would get similar answers from every other orphanage. He didn't know what to do, he was lost. It seemed that there was no help to wait for…

Despite nuns' rejection, he would still go to other orphanages. Even if he was rejected again, he still tried to look at the girls who were playing and learning in classes, hoping that maybe he would see a girl who resembled Maria. This was the same as looking for a needle in a haystack. Losing all hope, having gone through his whole list of orphanages and concluding that he would not be able to complete the countess' mission he found on the upper west side of Manhattan an orphanage which was located within a church. The abbess patiently listened to Adam's request and like the others said that there was no way she could help. But, as Adam was ready to leave, a nun came running into the office and said that she must talk to the abbess right away. The abbess apologized and asked Adam to wait in the room and left. Adam was examining the holy icons in the room, and one of the icons looked very unusual. He came closer to it to look at it better and accidentally eavesdropped on the conversation that was in the other room.

"Look at her," said one of the nuns to the abbess. "She doesn't want to wear the required uniform that every girl wears in our church. She keeps asking to wear that old, green dress of hers. It's not even fit to wear anymore."

Adam got worried and understood that if he opened the door and saw that there was a girl with green eyes then she would be the countess who he had been searching for. One step, the door slammed open, and he saw the back of a girl with brown wavy hair, in a green old dress whose color had faded, and was holding a black and white uniform in her hands. Adam wanted to believe that he had finally found her. The little girl, as if she felt it, slowly turned her face and, oh God, he saw a face that looked like Maria and with big, beautiful eyes which gleamed and sparkled with an unusual emerald green.

"I found her," said Adam and at this moment felt his feet tremble. He fell to the ground as if his whole body was soft cotton.

He awoke in a fog. The abbess couldn't believe Adam for a while and that he had found the girl that he was really looking for and as for the story about the deceased grandmother who gave him a request, he didn't even tell because he didn't want them to think he was crazy. He didn't know what to do, he felt even more hurt from the fact that he finally found her, but now he had to take her from the orphanage, somehow. For some reason the abbess asked

Adam, "How did you get the address of this orphan house? Usually people rarely come here, because we are the farthest away from downtown."

Adam started saying something about the bureau of information which gave him the address. He felt the paper with addresses in his pocket, and gave it to the abbess for no reason. The abbess took the list, put her glasses on and started reading it. Adam was getting surprised as how her face was changing.

"Oh great then," said the abbess. "This is alright with us. I think you can take the girl with you in the afternoon," and gave orders to the other nuns to gather all the girl's things together.

Adam couldn't understand what was going on. He asked to get the paper back from the abbess. He started reading it and saw that it was a letter from Maria Markovsky to pick up her grand-granddaughter from the orphanage and having Adam become the girl's legal guardian. At the bottom of the letter, there were all the requirements for the legal paper, plus a notary public and a last name of the notaries—Vivimas. Adam thought to himself, "Definitely, without the help of heaven's chancellery I wouldn't have able to solve this matter." The abbess told the little Countess that today she would leave the orphanage and go with Adam because her grandmother had asked him to take her.

"Will he allow me to wear only green dresses?" asked the little Countess.

"Of course," said Adam. "I cannot move against the traditions of many generations." He came closer to the little girl, bent a little and kindly asked, "What is your name?"

"She doesn't like to be called by her name," said a nun who was her teacher. "She likes when people call her by her nickname—Komissa."[1]

"Komissa, that's a pretty nickname. I will call you that then," kindly said Adam. "How old are you, Komissa?"

"I just turned twelve," said Komissa.

"Oh, you're not a little Countess anymore," said Adam

After a few hours, Adam came out from the gates of the church. In his left hand he was holding a little suitcase. In his right hand he was holding Komissa's hand. And with every step as they were leaving the church, Adam felt easier and happier from the fact that he had kept his promise. The bystanders who were looking at them were a bit confused because they wondered why such a well-dressed father had a beautiful daughter but in a very old and fading green dress.

NOTE

1. KOMISSA—from Greek means Countess.

Chapter Fourteen

Journey to the Castle

Day after day, Adam got used to his new role of being a father and a friend to Komissa. Of course after a few days, in Komissa's closet were a lot of outfits of green, which she adored. They matched her beautiful brown wavy hair and big green eyes. Adam wanted to tell her about what family she came from, but he knew that she might not be ready for that yet and a bit more time should pass.

The little girl started going to school and showed her talent in drawing, languages and music. On weekends, they mostly loved walking in Central Park and every time took a ride in a horse-drawn carriage. But their favorite thing to do was to find a special coachman; Adam found a coachman that looked like Amaxas. Sometimes, they would even stand in a line, just to ride with him; Adam wanted to experience the same feeling over again when he was riding on the Phaeton. He tried to tell Komissa about this unusual ride on the Phaeton, but every time he understood that for her this was no more than just a fairy tale. That's why every time he would add some fairy tale details and both would understand that it was just fantasy.

He saw that Komissa loved these stories about riding on the Phaeton and reaching the top of the blue sky where they got to meet angels who had different colored wings. Sometimes they would ask the coachman to drive faster, close their eyes, and sing a silly made-up song: "This is us on the Phaeton riding in the blue sky, we are happy, we enjoy the fun, and we enjoy the blue sky." Sometimes, Adam would forget, and call the coachman Max. At first the coachman wouldn't like that and say he had another name, but then he just got used to it. Plus, Adam and Komissa were his frequent clients and gave good tips. Adam was excited and happy, also because after some time the chairperson from his department was fired and the new chairperson was hiring people to work in a laboratory for grants and he viewed Adam as the best candidate. He was offered a part-time position in the same department but with a condition that after one year he would successfully conduct research. Adam was spending a lot of time in the laboratory and was really excited that he finally had the chance to realize all his ideas which he had been carrying in his mind for a long time.

However, a thought about Komissa's castle which she hadn't seen before didn't give him any peace. He really wanted to make a gift for her and show her this castle. Plus, Maria's soul, which was somewhere near his grandfather's soul would have been thankful to him. Adam thought, "How interestingly people's lives intersect. If it wasn't for Maria's precious stones, it was most likely that my grandfather wouldn't have been close to the invention which can cure the entire human race." Sometimes, when he would look at Komissa, who as a child played with dolls, he would think, "How powerful human genetics are, since with preciously green eyes, she also inherited the manners of a countess and a passion to wear green dresses, though no one could have told her about the habits of her family members. And habits, as was told in heaven's chancellery, never go away."

In autumn, Adam had a vacation and he thought this was the best time to go to Poland. Plus, from the first days as Komissa was living with Adam, she would tell him that every night she saw only one dream, but didn't want to tell him at first because when she told about it to the nuns, they laughed at her and said that it was just her fantasy. One day, Adam went to Komissa's room and saw that she was drawing something. When he came closer, he saw that she was hiding the picture with her hand. However, when he asked her to show him what she had drawn, she finally showed him and Adam saw that it was a beautiful castle in a European style.

"This is a beautiful castle, Komissa, Now, why would you hide it?" asked Adam.

"Because this is the castle from my dream. When I would tell the nuns and my friends that it's a real castle where I lived, everybody would laugh at me. Will you laugh at me too?" Komissa asked sadly and her eyes were filling up with tears.

"Of course not," said Adam and hugged the girl. "I know you are telling the truth. Plus, my little girl, I think it's time for you to really see this castle. I think the time has come for you to know the truth."

Then the little girl calmed down and they decided to have a picnic on the carpet. They decided to put all the pictures that Komissa drew on the floor. Adam was astonished with what talent she drew the details of the castle: the staircase, the columns, etc. They were having a snack, talking, and it was obvious that Komissa enjoyed this moment, since she finally found a person who would not laugh at her dreams. Adam asked her to tell him about her dream and after a few requests she began, "Sometimes I see the same dream.

It happened long time ago when I was very little. I have grown up, but I have the same dream. It never leaves."

"What do you see in your dream?" asked Adam and saw this as a genetic memory that was trying to express itself through her dreams.

"Sometimes I see myself somewhat like a princess and I live in a huge castle. I love the feeling that I am a princess. I know that I am a special princess because I always wear a beautiful green dress, sparkly jewelry with green stones. I look at myself in the mirror and twirl to see how beautiful my outfit is. I also like my new shiny shoes with small heels. You know why? Because when I run on the marble floor, I can hear them knocking as I make my steps. But the best thing I love is getting on the farthest part of the castle where grown-ups don't allow me to go alone. They say because the staircase there is very narrow and slippery. It has many tiny steps which lead somewhere up. But I find the chance when I can run away from everybody and am running to that side of the castle. I like that I disobeyed and am doing something that I'm not allowed to do. I start running up a vintage staircase. I feel so light as if I can fly. I hop from one stair to another so lightly that sometimes my toes don't even touch it, as if I'm flying. I feel as if my body is lightweight, but I still hear the sound of my heels. This way I'm going up and up and up. I am very curious what is up there. But when I almost get to reach the top, I always wake up, and I don't know what is up there," concluded Komissa.

Adam looked at Komissa so dearly, it seemed that Adam understood that Komissa was talking about a castle belonging to the dynasty of Count Markovsky and located somewhere very far away in Poland.

Then Adam responded, "You know, I am sure that you will see everything yourself pretty soon, and you'll see that your dream will be a reality."

Finally, one day Adam and Komissa full of desire began their adventure to Poland. Hours in an airplane weren't as exhausting as it sounded. However, to reach their destination, Adam and the little countess had to take a bus tour to get to the family castle of Markovsky. The bus slowly approached an old village which was close to Warsaw. It was full of tourists from various countries. Mostly they were elderly but energetic people who wore nice clothes: shorts, t-shirts and tennis shoes. It seemed as if even if they were tourists from various countries, it is as if they planned to wear the same thing or went to the same store and bought the same tennis shoes. Adam was surprised that even if they were elderly they were easily using modern technology. This seemed unusual because people at that age usually didn't like to use new high-technology. There were a lot of elderly couples, they were holding each other's hands so sweetly and there was certain jealous from Adam because they were able to hold on to their feelings and continue them through many years.

Men were trying to elegantly hold onto their women by the arm, while most women were wearing the same form and color of hairstyle. It seemed to Adam that their heads mostly looked like dandelions, the flowers withered and from a slight wind all petals might fly away. But, all these women had all their pedals on even if they were withered and luckily the wind didn't touch them. Adam was sitting in the bus, looking at the heads of these women and it seemed to him that these were many dandelions which were not withering even though it was autumn.

The tour guide was a young lady in her thirties of an unknown nationality. It was obvious that she spoke on many languages and due to her profession, she talked with a lot of people from various countries. That's why she talked with an accent and Adam knew that this often happened with people who knew more than one language. By looking at her, it seemed to Adam that a lot of cultures were able to fit into one person. It seemed to him that she looked more like a vase where you can place many tiny flags of various countries. Probably, because her body looked like a vase and she wore clothing from various cultures as if she was a vase filled with all these flags. He noticed the young lady always seemed worried and smoked at the bus stops. From this it seemed that every country whose language she knew smoked with her.

Later, the tour guide announced with a harsh voice that there was an old castle that had survived from the eighteenth century. As the bus climbed to the top of the hill Adam and the little Countess saw the sharply angled roofs of the castle; the roofs were amazing and resembled trees with golden leaves. There were a lot of trees, but they weren't tall, they mostly grew up to the middle of the castle; that was why from far away it seemed that the roofs of this castle were laying on the golden leaves. It felt as if this castle was weightless and the upper part of it was hanging between earth and the sky. But if one came closer, the trees were further apart and the castle was standing in its full length.

Then everybody was asked to get off the bus. Adam and his little Countess were the first to get off and went to see the castle. Komissa was calm since she was quite sleepy; it seemed that she still couldn't understand that they finally reached the surprise which Adam had promised to her. The little girl felt that Adam was quite nervous; she was looking around and saw that there was nothing to worry about; while Adam would nervously cough, in order to make him feel a little better, she would hold his hand very tightly.

After a few minutes, before the tourists stood a castle with ancient cracked walls. These cracks looked like wrinkles on the face of the castle. Still the items in the castle had been nicely preserved. They saw a big table with strong legs. Around the table there were a couple of chairs that looked like thrones. At that moment Komissa imagined she was sitting on one of those thrones and thought how hard it would be to sit all day with a straight back. The whole group was going over to see a knight's armor when something attracted Komissa's attention in the next room.

In that room she enjoyed a lot of old paintings, one of which was particularly interesting to her. When she and Adam went closer they were shocked with the image. In the painting there was a young woman that looked just like her. She was wearing an amazing green dress with a high neck in an old fashioned style. Also she had on old fashioned earrings and a necklace that were green. This lady had brown wavy hair and a wide forehead. For them the most amazing thing was her unbelievably emerald green eyes. Under the portrait there was a name tag which said that her name was Countess Miroslawa Markowski, a member of one of the dynasties of the owners of this castle.

Adam and Komissa were standing in front of the portrait for a few minutes and couldn't say a word. Adam understood that Komissa was in her own castle where her ancestors used to live. Komissa was shocked but she also understood that the woman on the portrait was somehow related to her and slowly said to Adam, "Look, this woman on the portrait is also wearing a green dress, just how I like to."

Because she is your relative," said Adam "Yes, this woman may be your grand-grand-grandmother."

Komissa loudly laughed at his answers and said, "Oh, this is another fairy tale which you're telling me."

"No," said Adam. "Close your eyes and remember in your pictures, where was the staircase located?"

"Over there," she said, pointing to another end of the hallway where the tourists were standing with the tour lady.

Adam looked where Komissa was pointing and saw that the hallway was ending with a red drape that was covering the end of the hallway with a sign saying "No entrance allowed."

"Let's not be law-abiding," said Adam. He took Komissa by hand and they rushed to the end of the hallways so that the tour lady wouldn't see them.

"Here on the right side, towards the end should be a staircase which leads to the top," said Komissa. "Yes, yes, I see it, I see it. Hurry, look how many stairs there are," she exclaimed.

Adam was more and more sure how realistic Komissa's dreams were. Truly, they soon got to a narrow hallway with a staircase that led to one of the towers. The staircase was swirling up with many tiny marble stairs. The walls of this tower were made of materials that looked like bricks but made out of rock. The marble stairs in most places were slightly ruined and had cracked tips. Adam and Komissa were going higher and higher and Komissa though didn't hear the sound of her heels at every step, still was as excited as she was in her dream. "A few more steps, only three, two…" thought Komissa and she finally reached the last step of the staircase and got to the top of this tower. Adam hurried after her and also reached the top of the tower. They both saw that on top of the tower was a small playground which was surrounded by a fence with pointed ends.

"Oh, finally I found out what was at end of this staircase," happily exclaimed Komissa.

"Yes, we are on the roof of the castle," said Adam.

Then after some time as they were hugging, they were enjoying the view from the tower, but from this height they could only see the golden leaves of the trees. They were able to see the full beauty of autumn which were around the whole castle. It seemed that at this moment, time lost its value. Adam finally felt peace and calmness in his soul, that he was able to complete Maria's request, and that he did something good for Markovsky's dynasty that were unfairly ruined by the Communists. Then after they came to themselves, they understood that they have to go back with the tourists. They easily went downstairs and momentarily were part of the tourists and were glad that no one noticed them going away. The elderly tourists were saying that was time for them to go and that they were exhausted, while the tour lady was arguing with the curator because there was no place for her to smoke.

From the tour lady and the supervisors of this castle Adam couldn't get any explanation about the woman in the portrait. However, for Komissa and Adam there was no doubt that they were finally able to get closer to the secret held for centuries.

Chapter Fifteen

Justice Served

After returning from Poland, Adam felt relieved. His friendship with Komissa was only getting better and he finally found a kind soul to be with. He knew that his hearing in heaven's chancellery which was suddenly given to him, gave him an opportunity not only to get closer to the tragedy of Markovsky's family, but also understand the importance of his invention. Before, he knew that he didn't have anything but to continue working on the invention which his grandfather had started. However, now, after many things had cleared out, in what environment and reasons his grandfather started the invention, how poor Maria gave her life because of her family treasure which she wanted so as to serve the people, grandfather's invention and Maria's precious stones helped to treat a number of soldiers; however, these people don't exist anymore, but the idea still does. Now, on another end of the world, again, two representatives from the same generation, Adam as the next generation from his grandfather, was continuing to work on the invention, and Maria's granddaughter Komissa, who inspired him to work on the invention. From all these thoughts, Adam's head was spinning, he felt like the chosen one and was sure that the little countess was also chosen and it was not by chance that they had met. "How weird, how weird…" thought Adam. "In order for an invention that helps people to work, many people have to die in tragic circumstances no matter in what time period. It can be in World War II under Stalin's power, or in peaceful modern America with people who only worry about money. Maybe these people have to sacrifice themselves in order to help thousands of people to survive…"

Adam was very enthusiastic about his job and spent many days in his laboratory and knew that Komissa was waiting for him at home. She had lost her parents when she was little and that's why she didn't know maternal or paternal care. She liked that Adam never laughed when she would draw her dreams or other fantastic ideas which before seemed very unreal to people. Now she understood what genetic memory was and that it was a special gift which she got from previous generations. Before she used to worry that she was an orphan and didn't have what other children had who live with families. Now she knew that she had Adam, she had a special gift and knowledge and talent from generations which were saved in her memory and in the blood flowing through her whole body.

After a year of hard work, Adam was finally able to restore the sketch of the invention and also some parts of his machine. Of course, he updated many things after his grandfather's invention and of course, his grandfather's first sketches were too simple after what Adam did. Later, Adam's monograph was published and an article about the potential of the invention which healed people by using precious stones. The new chairman loved Adam's work and he would praise him and soon Adam received a full-time position. Adam was excited and after a few months his presentation was scheduled in one of the conferences in Europe. Actually, similar inventions were already researched in various countries of the world and Adam was very curious how far did they had gone with their inventions.

The day when Adam received an invitation to the conference, in the hallway he saw the previous chairman Mr. Ali Baster and it was obvious to Adam that he looked very weird. His pathos and haughtiness disappeared. Instead, Adam saw a hunched, almost bald man with no spark in his eyes. He would guiltily look around and it seemed as if Ali Baster even got shorter. Before, Adam viewed him as a strong and powerful enemy, but now looked like an innocent and pitiful man. They passed each other in the hallway and their eyes met for a second. "Oh, this is the meeting in the Elbe," thought Adam. Though Ali Baster just passed Adam and tried not to look at him. Adam's assistant, who was walking next to him, also felt pity for Ali Baster and said to Adam, "Yes, it was hard for Ali Baster in the last year. He was on treatment with a shrink for a while, but it was unsuccessful."

"With a shrink?" asked Adam

"Oh, you don't know?! After a couple of months when he was fired from his job he was evaluated to be mentally insane. Ali Baster's colleagues and relatives began to notice his weird behavior. Can you believe it, he was scared to go back to sleep, because he would say that during sleep he could be kidnapped and questioned by heaven's chancellery which would view his aura..."

Adam just loudly laughed in response. His assistant expected that, since it was really a funny story about Ali Baster. However, Adam was very surprised because he was sure that only he would remember visiting heaven's chancellery. He remembered everything in detail, though a lot of time had passed. He thought this was his privilege because he was invited to a hearing on the seventh level, by the summons, officially and was very excited that he was the only one who had that chance. To not just speak on the heaven's chancellery, but also remember what had happened there. However, as he understood, Ali Baster also had memories of visiting the heaven's chancellery, but it seemed that the biggest punishment for Ali Baster was that every truth which he would tell people about heaven's chancellery, people viewed absurd. "Oh, I guess no matter in what court you are, on earth or in heaven, it matters on what end of the court you are. You are a plaintiff or a defendant, you won the case or you lost it. From this depends your whole life, your place on earth and then later in heaven, thought Adam. "Oh, God, how hard this is." It seemed that the assistant didn't notice Adam being in thought and just continued telling his funny story, "...and can you believe it, he threw away his favorite baby blue pajamas and would say that you were the reason he was mentally sick and that he is innocent. Oh you know, when Ali Baster was still working in our laboratory, I once saw how he was panicking when he was coming close to the invention. I honestly don't get Ali Baster," the assistant concluded his story. "Why did he return to work back in our University after the treatment? You see, he started working as a custodian and not a very good one. I see he is always alone and mostly likes to sit and talk to guinea pigs and mice for hours, and doesn't notice that people are laughing at him."

But no matter how the assistant tried to tell a funny story about Ali Baster, it didn't seem funny to Adam. He was a bit upset that the defendants who were in heaven's chancellery actually had a memory of being there. He got upset about and thought that it might even be dangerous. That's why the first thing he did was to find as much information as possible about the journalist Lampoon.

For a few days he was researching online. He talked to a few reporters and finally found out the following: Mr. Lampoon very enthusiastically tried to make money on T.V. He even started his own show which he called "Only the Truth about Heaven's Chancellery." In this show he tried to prove to people that he was the only one special person in the world who had a chance to go on a trial in the seventh level of heaven's chancellery; only he would know a unique procedure conducted in court that is very different from earthly courts. He even drew a sketch of how the courtroom looked. He would tell where the judges sat, how the expertise was conducted, and he drew two marble stands one bigger than the other. The first few shows seemed funny to people. They thought that it was just his interesting imagination. In the next shows where he said that he saw Themis actually judging with open eyes and didn't have any scales, people viewed this as him throwing a challenge to the whole judicial system. Because of that the agency received phone calls from many court participants who would state that he was discrediting the judicial system. But Lampoon was not giving up, he would actively continue stating that he was right and in one of his shows he even brought his favorite underwear with the dollar prints and the cap with a golden tassel. He tried to prove that in this underwear he was in heaven's chancellery as a defendant because he published one of the articles; and the cap he took away from one of the court participants, but he didn't know his name. Lampoon would state that he also wanted to take his mantle as well in order not to be naked in front of the court but couldn't. He even stated that an expertise should be done on this cap, and would argue that this cap was made out of a material that didn't exist on earth. But unfortunately, none of the laboratories agreed to conduct such an expertise. Some viewers enjoyed this show because it seemed very piquant for the defendant in court to be only in his underwear. These viewers expected something more to the story related with eroticism and sex between the court participants. But not getting such further development in the story they lost their interest. Most viewers viewed this show to be an absurd situation and a mocking of the court. After a couple of shows, it was canceled and Lampoon didn't make a fortune from it, so he had to return to work at the newspaper and got only a bad reputation from his show. For some time, Lampoon worked in a small newspaper which mostly published advertisements. However, he didn't find his luck here either. The problem was that if the newspaper published his article, then after some time the paper would turn yellow. At first, the editors would argue with the paper dealers, but then they realized that when Lampoon's article was not printed, then the newspaper was fine; and so Lampoon was fired from this job and wasn't hired by any others either. Hence, he was still actively searching for a job at any newspaper. People even had a nickname for him, "a journalist of a yellow paper." After finding all this information, Adam was calm because as he expected even if people had the memory of going to heaven's chancellery, others wouldn't believe them and would view them as crazy; and most importantly, knowledge about heaven's chancellery couldn't be utilized by people, and they couldn't make money from it. Heaven's chancellery kept this practice of the court procedure and knowledge which in no way possible could fit the values which existed on earth.

Chapter Sixteen

Adam's Triumph

Being part of the conference had changed Adam's life in a positive way. After many years of hard work on the invention, then after an embarrassing period of dragging in earthly courts, thanks to heaven's chancellery getting his possibility to work on the invention back, Adam finally reached what he dreamed of for the last few years. At the conference, Adam was not just able to show his possibilities but found out many interesting things from other researches that created similar inventions and used precious stones to treat injuries as well. He was able to meet a couple of researchers and some of them shared their personal life stories. Adam was surprised how each of them in the beginning of their road to success faced rejection, were humbled, etc. They were all from different countries, but their stories were as if written by one author.

Adam was mostly surprised by the scientists from Russia who also presented their invention on treating the injured. It was based on the description of soldiers who took part in World War II. The researchers stated that a few of elderly people who came to their laboratory told them about a machine which sent a beam on a precious stone, through which they were able to heal when they were badly injured during the war. These personal stories the researchers used as a basis to work on their invention. But the fact that mostly astonished Adam was that among these soldiers, there were a few people who stated that they were about 100 years old, though they really looked in their twenties. They stated that after being under treatment of this machine, their injuries not only healed, but they felt younger. It seemed that they had stopped at this age. They didn't have elderly sicknesses. This was hard to believe too and many participants suspiciously listened to these statements; many of them stated that changing the age in the documents was easy and plus many documents could have been lost during the war or printed with mistake.

However, Russian researchers brought blood work reports of the family members of these soldiers who also came to the conference. An oddity of this case was that the children and grandchildren and wives of these soldiers looked way older than themselves. The DNA proved that they were related, and in order to conclude if they were speaking the truth, relatives and soldiers allowed for the researchers to see their DNA in laboratories of other countries. They wanted to prove that they were speaking the truth and work on the invention should be continued, but the researchers didn't have enough funds and for now people looked at them as mentally insane. Many aspects of the invention were so far just in monographs, theoretical and discussed in presentations. Adam understood that researchers from Russia and the supporting group which came with them spoke the truth, but he couldn't stand and speak in their support, because then he would have had to tell about going to the heaven's chancellery; but he already saw people's reaction when Ali Baster and Lampoon shared their stories.

However, after returning from the conference, in Europe, he understood that he was getting closer and closer to creating an invention which would be able to heal a large number of injured. He just wasn't sure whether the treatment would leave any side effects. In today's time, he only knew that the side effects of this invention were only positive and that by using a diamond then people not only could look younger, but could possibly be immortal. Did the human race need that? For many hours he was sitting in his office and grasped the fact that he was getting closer to the world's grand opening. In his head he saw relatives of these soldiers, while they were young, full of life and potency; and their grandchildren who were older, filled with human sadness and illness—the way all mortal people were. It seemed that fathers would bury their wives, children, grandchildren, "is that normal?" thought Adam. "Should I get involved in a standard and normal way of events, going against every human's normal routine of life?" It seemed that now Adam understood why every time, in different times, when his grandfather and he, himself were close to finishing working on the invention, some events or people would always intervene and have a hold up to develop the invention. In these moments, Adam would take his head in his hands, and just thoughtlessly look at one spot. Finally, after many months of arguing with himself, Adam was able to receive a patent on using his invention. One of the hospitals of New York agreed to use his machine and Adam was relieved that an invention which his grandfather started could finally be beneficial for people.

For many months, the invention was working miraculously and many clients were only getting better. Word about a "magical" machine was spreading across the country. Soon hospital was filled with people coming from other states. So many people wanted to be treated by the machine that not even the hospital and the nearby hotels were able to hold so many people. A few transportation companies thought of how to help people and at the same time make their money. They would suggest moving people to farther hotels by a bus and bring them to the hospital for treatment. Since there were a lot of people willing to try it out, the transportation companies were able to make a fortune. Both the mayor and the governor of New York were only for it because before they worried about a huge number of people crowding around the hospital and were afraid that it might cause riots and meetings. Even if they were sending a lot of police officers, still people were able to put up tents right on the sidewalk of the hospital. People would state that they would sleep there in order to be the first ones in line to get to the invention and get treated.

The advertisement companies were also making their way to the invention. They created various souvenirs, T-shirts, key chains, miniature statues, and even toys which looked like a machine that beamed a laser on a tiny crystal. All of these souvenirs were popular and getting swiftly bought not only by tourists but also New Yorkers. One of the jewelry companies even created a necklace with an image of this machine and a crystal. Giving such a necklace as a present was becoming a new trend among young people.

Many letters started coming as thanks to the hospital's address, doctors' addresses as well as Adam's address. People would write that they started feeling better, their quality of life got better, a lot of families got back together, a better relationship developed between parents and their children, people were able to return to their jobs; and of course Adam was speechlessly happy. Komissa was happy with him and childlike was caring for each of these letters, and she would file them accurately in Adam's office. Adam was very, very happy, but after giving much thought, he didn't decide to give away the secret of using a diamond in this machine.

Chapter Seventeen

The Secret Archive of Heaven's Chancellery

Adam was spending nights in his office twirling diamonds in his hands; he was pondering whether to use them in the invention; in the secret archive of heaven's chancellery (SAHC) was already a well-planned solution which Adam couldn't have known about. From the day of creation of heaven's chancellery, a secret archive was created which only a few participants knew about. It was a small place which was located not in basement of the building where it usually is on earth; that is, it wasn't a gray, old, dark place which smelled of rats' feces and dampness. In the heaven's chancellery it was decided to be a bit cleverer and the secret archive was hidden in another dimension. They opened a little bit more dimension in the hallways of heaven's chancellery and hid it there in a niche.

Millions of workers and the invited participants from earth would pass it a thousand times and would never notice it. Though, the "we know everything" Granny-Boxes, permanent court participants and their friends, partly predicted the existence of such an archive and secretly dreamed of peeking into it. Of course, it is obvious that no one was able to peek at it, even with a quarter of an eye, and the only thing that was left for them was to amuse themselves with their predictions. But even if they talked about it, the information about the secret archive was usually small, very broad and unclear.

When the Granny-Boxes talked about the secret archive, their faces were filled with seriousness, their eyes would become as round as spoons and they would always talk in whispers.

They would mostly say that it's very hard to get to the archive and if people would accidentally get there, then they would disappear similarly as people would disappear after visiting the KGB in Russia. One time there was a bit of gossip that an attorney from the civil court accidentally entered the archives and he disappeared for a time. Then later he was found to be an attorney on the family court level. When one of the Granny-Boxes saw him alive and well, she also found out that he was happy with his new position. She asked him, "How is the secret archive?" After which the attorney looked at her with amazement and said, "I don't know what you are talking about."

However, all the people who used to know this attorney said that he became very different and weird because every time he'd walk in the hallways, he was afraid of walking near one of the walls and would strictly walk in the center line.

In reality, the secret archive was placed on boring, grey shelves standing one after the next, in perfect rows and in accurately placed folders. On each folder was a sign which classified the secrecy of information in the folder. Basically, there were folders which were really secret and others not so much. In the farthest corner of the archive was a safe which contained folders with not just the top-secret cases but also on some of these folders there was a specific date of when the information contained could be publically displayed.

Neither Adam nor any court participants, not even judge Kumbi, could have thought that Adam's folder was placed precisely in this safe. The fact that Adam's grandfather Nicholas, without giving much thought, came very close to an invention which would give humanity something that the heaven's chancellery was afraid of sharing with people – immortality.

Honestly, before Nicholas, there were other scientists who were getting close to discovering the secret. But all the time, people from heaven would be sent down to earth or the line of events would get mixed up by the hands of heaven's chancellery, so that no one would discover the secret. Most of the time the mission would be successfully completed and a folder of this incident would be stocked in the archive. There were different time periods, scientists, people, tools that were used to stop the secret from being discovered, but the main subject was always the same.

Before, in heaven's chancellery no one thought that Nicholas would able to find precious stones for his invention, especially, during the war. The probability for Maria Markovsky to meet Nicholas was minimal. That's why, before, heaven's chancellery didn't have any reasons to worry about this. However, the first and every other medical experiments of treating the injuries occurred and something had to be done.

Then, people from heaven's chancellery were dressed as KGB officers and sent down to earth to confiscate this invention and destroy it. In order for everything to seem realistic, they had to shoot Maria Markovsky and send the doctors to Siberian camps. The doctor who was part of the experiment and a few soldiers who not only were treated but also got younger and immortal, it was decided on one of the meetings to let them be, because they knew that people would still not believe them because they were not ready for such phenomenon.

In the time when the supervisor was managing Nicholas' case in SAHC, he couldn't have thought that Nicholas would survive after such unbelievable conditions. Also, when by luck he came to US, he wanted to restore his invention and pass all his knowledge to his son. In the beginning of the 70's, his son, Adam's father, continued working on the invention and developed it further and made a few more steps to discovering what people shouldn't know about.

Then in the '70's, young, handsome Nicholas' son could have been very successful in science, especially in the US, because during that time it was encouraging such inventions and giving monetary support since the country wanted to prove, especially to its main opponent, the Soviet Union, that it was superior. Then the representatives of heaven's chancellery had nothing to do but to cause a car accident involving him and his wife.

For some time, in the secret archive, everybody calmed down because Adam was a child then and no one ever thought that he would continue working on the invention. But still the representatives of SAHC would watch him. That's why when Adam started working on the invention in the laboratory of the New York University, every day there would be a representative from SAHC who was invisible on earth. When Adam was working with various precious stones, the representative didn't mind and was even glad that finally Adam could create an invention thanks to which humanity would able to cure certain illness that were impossible to cure before. However, when Adam chose the right beam of light in the invention and pushed it on a diamond, it was a sign that it was time to stop him working on the invention.

Since Adam reached this development of the invention in the twenty-first century, KGB officers seemed irrelevant, and it was impossible for Adam to have a car accident because he didn't have a car; that's why the representatives of SAHC had to use the most common tool in New York—jealousy. That's why Ali Baster got very jealous of Adam's success. And as people say in heaven's chancellery, you just have to spread jealousy among people and they'll do the rest. Hence, the representatives of SAHC didn't waste their energy and time to cause moral damage to Adam, or plagiarize his work, slander him, and commit arson in the laboratory; Ali Baster did everything for them. This time as before, representatives of SAHC prevented people from finding out the secret of immortality; they were doing their job very well.

However, this time, Adam without giving it much thought, asked for compensation in heaven's chancellery for moral damage in the right place and time; that's why his request was approved. During a couple of months, there was tension between the seventh level of heaven's chancellery, where Adam's petition was sent, and the representative of SAHC. Even if Themis was taking part in this issue a couple of times, the SAHC was still standing its ground. When the due date on Adam's folder came, it meant that it was time for people to receive a new invention; it was decided to approve Adam's petition. However, due to consensus an unusual decision was made. If Adam won the case, then it would be up to him to decide the fate of human immortality.

Honestly, opinions on this matter opposed one another. Knowing the tragedy of Adam's family who suffered from this invention, Themis believed that Adam would decide to open the secret of immortality for people. The representatives of SAHC, in contrast, believed that Adam, having seen a handful of injustices in the world, as well as in his family, would never decide to reveal the secret.

However, what's the point of guessing? The decision was made which was that Adam's memory would not be erased after the hearing and besides receiving compensation for his moral damage—a sixth sense—he would also make a decision of how to get around with the secret of immortality.

Chapter Eighteen

Meanwhile in Heaven's Chancellery

Meanwhile, Heaven's Chancellery continued its usual way of life. The seventh level was one of the busiest levels as usual, but at the same time, this court couldn't be considered overcrowded. They continued following their strict rule—one hearing per day. As usual, before the entrance, the sisters Vivimas would hang an announcement about who would be the judge to review the hearing and whose case would be heard. Due to that, in the last days word spread around the heaven's chancellery that it was not a good practice to have the court hearing reviewed by only one judge—a hearing with one judge and his two assistants. For a while now, new prepositions were suggested for the seventh level to have a couple of other judges. No one was personally against Kumbi as a candidate and his two assistants Synaisthema and Mello, because there was no question of a mistrial. However, the fact that the decision on the seventh level was always done by only one judge, may have caused court participants from other levels to have second thoughts. No doubt those influential judges from other levels and who knew Kumbi stated that moral damage was a specific damage and to find other candidates for a judge was very hard. That's why everything should be left as it was. Though they knew that in other levels, for example, where civil cases were reviewed, or criminal cases, family cases, administrative cases, environmental protection cases always had variations of judges and their assistants. Time passed, centuries passed, but no one was willing enough to change the procedure in the seventh level of heaven's chancellery. Plus, all the court participants in this level knew each other for a while now; they were a team and conducted all the procedures smoothly.

After the hearing of Adam's case, certain things changed in the courtroom. No, nothing changed in regards to the procedures or the schedules, but among the individual lives of court participants, because as we noticed before, they were as human as they could be. Even during Adam's case, some chatter-boxes noticed that counsel Coeus was indifferent to Arianna and most people started observing this couple at each hearing. People even started making predictions. Granny-Boxes were mostly involved in the gossip because they didn't have their own love-life to handle; they could at least talk about someone else's. They thought that observing a real-life relationship was way more interesting than watching a soap-opera. And then at one hearing they noticed that Arianna kindly smiled to Coeus, then at another hearing, Coeus gently touched Arianna's elbow, at the third hearing they said that Coeus and Arianna were nicely talking to each other during a break at the buffet; then even one of the grannies who lately was worried about hearing problems, was able to hear that Coeus and Arianna were planning a date.

It seemed that during these weeks, the progress in the love relationship of this couple was vitally important more than the cases that were heard. But since we weren't there, we can't really say if it is true or not. However, calmer court participants saw that after a couple of months, Arianna and Coeus in the morning came to the hearing together in one Phaeton and even had breakfast together in the cafeteria.

But moving on from the lovely couple, then there was louder news that spread around the courtroom and took the attention of the chatter-boxes. It was said that one of the members of the audience was a good friend of the bailiff and supposedly when the friend was having another drink with the bailiff, he told him that he saw that everyday Kumbi was sewing on buttons on his mantle. Supposedly, he saw that in front of Kumbi there was a big box filled with a sewing kit. At first, no one really believed the witness of this event, because everybody knew that the bailiff had a habit of drinking and may have imagined it. However, the bailiff was so intensely swearing that he was telling the truth, that many people started believing him. To the stories about Kumbi more stories started coming up about other judges from different levels. For example, a judge from the family court was a woman who had the habit of picking houses online as if she was going to buy them. This habit she got when she lived on earth and she still couldn't get over. People say when she lived on earth, no matter what jobs she worked at, she still couldn't save money for a down payment to buy a house in New York, and hence, she passed away before achieving her dream; while the judge from the criminal level had a habit of shopping online. The problem was, for his home address he was writing "Sixth Level of Heaven's Chancellery—Temple of Justice." And if you can believe it, in time he received a delivery from China, though with an extended delivery process, but he got to receive it. Court participants enjoyed a good laugh about these stories, and they loved re-telling them and adding their own details to them.

One day, this gossip reached Kumbi himself, and do you think he got embarrassed? No. During breaks or when he had free time, he would sit in an open space, take a sewing kit, and start sewing buttons on his mantle. Can you imagine the faces of the gossips? They didn't have anything else to say about Kumbi. Then they stopped talking about him altogether. So, they started talking about the prosecutor Ipsos. His health condition was always worrying the heaven's chancellery. The fact that he was scared of heights wasn't a secret to anyone. However, people were worried that Ipsos started going to Pilates courses. Well, what is so surprising about it? I would only be happy for him. But the court participants were worried that Ipsos would forget to change and come in his gym clothes right to the hearing. At the last moment he would put on his mantle and a cap, but still looked weird because he would have sneakers on. Can you imagine, once he came to the hearing with a rolled yoga-mat on his back which he had used during Pilates. He forgot to take it off and was sitting and wearing it at the preliminary hearing, until Kumbi gave him a warning.

But the most surprising factor was Themis' behavior. After Adam came down to earth, she started looking for various excuses to get down to earth as well. She started spending more hours in the library, learning about earthly cases, laws, and as usual she didn't like most of the things which took place in earthly courts. Before, she was calm, but now she became more perky and wasn't shy anymore to directly speak out her dislike of certain earthly laws. She would always say that policies should be changed in the court procedures in earthly courts, for example, policies should be changed regarding selective incapacitation because it was not effective for reducing serious crime. Another day, she said that people on earth should abolish the three strikes law because it is inhumane. Then she stated that the time came to have bail reform. The only thing which pleased her a little was that people finally started using DNA as sufficient evidence. Themis even said: "Thank God, that on earth there is finally the Innocence Project and now thousands of innocent people will be exonerated. Plus, these were cases regarding serious felony cases such as murder and rape." Basically she talked about difficult legal terms which not all court participants would understand and would just quietly stand and nod their heads so that she wouldn't get more upset. One day she was very upset about the fact that one of the laws was not being followed on earth regarding a speedy trial. She was so upset that she was even ready to go down on earth. Some of her friends even saw that she had already packed her luggage and was about to order the Phaeton. Thankfully, on her way, Coeus saw her and was able to talk her out of going on her unusual trip. Coeus was very knowledgeable about women's psychology. You of course are curious of what did he tell her that she changed her mind. He just simply asked her; did she think that her bright azure, loose-fitting dress was appropriate for an earthly court? Themis curiously asked why her dress would be inappropriate. To which Coeus answered that traditionally, in earthly courts, people came in strict business suits and not elegant dresses.

After which, Themis lost her vibe and said, maybe Coeus was right, she didn't have any strict business suits, that was why she wouldn't be able to provide justice on earth. Of course, Coeus was glad that he was able to talk Themis out of going. Continuing the subject he said that people on earth weren't used to seeing Themis without a blindfold, and a sword and a shield. Themis quickly agreed and thought that this absurdity would remain on earth for a while. After which she confidently walked back to the Temple of Justice. Of course, nothing finished after that. Themis still had failed tries to get down on earth. That's why heaven's inhabitants see Themis with a suitcase, they know that she is not going anywhere; she is just very upset and worried about another aspect of an earthly courts. Usually, in these cases she felt embarrassed and would say to people, "oh, it's better for people to come here."

Epilogue

One day, Adam found an unusual post-card in his mailbox; there were beautiful blue irises drawn on it and it said that it was "From: Themis" and the return address was "Temple of Justice," followed by only a few words: "Congrats for your success." Adam took that as a sign and would always carry this card with him. One night, when he was returning home, he saw a woman who carried a bouquet with lilac irises. The young lady was surprised when Adam took out the post-card which had the same flowers she carried. She told him, "Do you too like lilac irises?" and he said, "Well, not really, it's just that it's a sign to me from heaven." The young woman smiled and said, "I own a flower shop, we grow a lot of flowers, but we mostly specialize in irises, we send them across the world."

In the evening, Adam and his new friend went on a date. After a couple of months, he proposed to her and gave her a ring which did not have a diamond, but a blue tanzanite.

I don't know what will happen to them next, but just before this book was published, I saw them all in Central Park. Three happy people who were holding hands: a handsome young man, a happy young woman, and between them a precious young girl. They passed me and were so happy that they didn't notice anybody. When they went a little further, I looked at them and walked with peace.

www.ingramcontent.com/pod-product-compliance
Lightning Source LLC
Chambersburg PA
CBHW020944310726
48980CB00001B/46

* 9 7 8 0 7 6 1 8 6 4 5 2 3 *